SOME
ASSEMBLY
REQUIRED

Discovering God's Plans for Your Life

ANDRÉ BLYTHE

EMPOWERMENT
PRESS

Published by Empowerment Press

ebook: 979-8-9916165-0-8
Paperback: 979-8-9916165-1-5

Praise for *Some Assembly Required*

"The assembly of experiences shared in this book molded the man we see today, and it is the ordained work of our Father in heaven. Life is a series of events that mold our reference point of how effective and fulfilling our lives are to others. André's determination and faith through life-altering events remind us that with man alone, things are impossible, but with God, all things are possible. This book will remind any person facing seemingly insurmountable challenges that they can trust Jesus. Whether the challenges are in their marriages, careers, or family, they can trust Jesus' plans because He will bring them through."

CARLOS COLEMAN
Lead Pastor, New Eirth Outreach Church, Midland, Georgia

"It is an honor to endorse my good friend, André Blythe, and his powerful new book, *Some Assembly Required: Discovering God's Plans for Your Life*. Having had the pleasure of working alongside André in ministry and witnessing his extraordinary teaching gift, I can truly say this book reflects the life of a man who practices what he preaches and writes about. His insights on how the Lord can work mightily in the lives of those who commit to follow Him are both practical and inspiring. *Some Assembly Required* has personally motivated and challenged me in my own walk with Christ, and I highly recommend it to anyone seeking to discover God's plans for their life."

LEE ALLEN JENKINS
Senior Pastor, Eagles Nest Church, Roswell, Georgia

"In *Some Assembly Required* my dear friend André Blythe not only gives us an inviting call to order our lives according to God's plans, but he shows us how this can be accomplished. Written through the lens of his own journey and experience, André applies the principles found in Jeremiah Chapter 29 in a wonderfully compelling way. I love this book. If you want to know and experience God's plans for your life, then *Some Assembly Required* is the book for you."

DR. CRAWFORD W. LORITTS, JR.
Author, Speaker, Radio Host,
Founder and President of Beyond our Generation

"André Blythe's *Some Assembly Required: Discovering God's Plan for You*r Life is a transformative masterpiece that speaks to the soul and ignites the spirit. With profound insight and relatable anecdotes, Blythe masterfully guides readers like a tour guide on a journey to uncover their divine purpose. Each page is a blend of wisdom and inspiration, making it impossible to put down. A must-read for anyone seeking clarity and deeper connection with God's plan for their life!"

DR. CRAIG L OLIVER,
Elizabeth Baptist Church, Atlanta, Georgia

To my wife and partner Leslie:

Thank you for your love and support during this thirty-five-year journey through life. We have enjoyed mountaintop experiences, grown through valley experiences, and weathered storms together. God has used them all to strengthen us for this next season of life. The way you ministered to your late mom and stepfather from May 2023–May 2024 was amazing to see. God really used you to show His presence and love. I love you!

To our son Myles:

It has been my absolute pleasure and privilege to teach, guide, provide for, correct, and prepare you to live this life as a young adult and to set you on course to walk the path of God's calling for you. God has planted His joy, love, and compassion in you through Jesus Christ, and He will use them to indelibly impact your sphere of influence. I love you!

To my parents: the late Anel and Jessie Blythe

Neither of my parents had much of a childhood. Both of them had adult responsibilities thrust upon them before they were ready to assume them, yet they pressed through. Dad and Mom did the best they knew how to raise us, and I am forever grateful. Other than my relationship with God, their influence and what I learned from their lives gave me a strong foundation. Love and miss you both!

CONTENTS

PART ONE

Discovering God's Plans Requires That You Prepare Practically

JEREMIAH 29:5-9

HOW DID I GET HERE FROM THERE?

I t was June of 1978. The graduation stage. Spartanburg High School in Spartanburg, S.C.

I can hear some of you already asking, "Where in the *world* is Spartanburg, S.C.?" and I understand why. But I am proud to be from Spartanburg, to be the son of the late Anel and Jessie Blythe, and the third from the youngest of eight children—William, Anita, Margie, Michael, Zarita, Pamela, Patrick, and me.

In high school, I was usually a B student, with some As and Cs sprinkled in there. I was smart, but I had trouble staying focused. Sports were my passion—I loved playing basketball, football, baseball, and tennis—and while I was an athlete (and remain athletic to this day), there were far better athletes than I on these teams.

I had been quite an introvert until my 12th-grade year, but I finally fought my way out of the cocoon of shyness. That year, I was scheduled to graduate early, so I had the opportunity to take several electives. And there they were—classes about business. They captured my attention, and I began to dream about being in business because it seemed very natural and exciting to me.

In August 1978, I started my Business Administration degree pursuit at the University of South Carolina-Spartanburg (now USC Upstate) while working part-time and living at home.

FROM FAILURE TO SUCCESS

I must be totally honest here. Between the young ladies, having fun, and hanging out with friends, by the beginning of my sophomore year I got really distracted. While I had been raised to have a *religious respect* for God and Jesus Christ, *I absolutely had no relationship with Him,* and I certainly lived that way.

Then, a catalyst for change came: my dad had a stroke, and he had to stop working part-time (he was a retired gourmet chef who helped lead the Guest House Staff at Milliken Research Corporation). The entire financial weight of the house now fell on my mom, and a level of stress we had not seen before settled on our family.

I decided to find a full-time job and change my day classes to nights and weekends. I was not very disciplined in most parts of my life, except for work, so this was really challenging for me. Before long, I had quit college and was really enjoying being a Manager Trainee at a national retail chain store. My decision to quit college broke my mother's heart, but I promised her that I would one day go back and earn my degree. My dad didn't want me to quit college either, but he started to see his once introverted son blossom into a young businessman.

On the day that he died in July of 1982, one of his best friends, our life insurance agent—the late Mr. Wofford—pulled me aside and shared how proud my dad was of me. He shared that they talked about me every time he stopped by to collect the life insurance payment. That filled my heart then and still makes me smile now.

I thrived in learning every aspect of operating the retail store.

In less than a year, I was the Store Manager at nineteen years old! I absolutely loved recruiting and developing employees, merchandising the store, selling the merchandise, and building great client relations. My dream now shifted to opening my own store one day—that would be the epitome of success for me! I would later transfer to lead much larger stores in the Washington, DC and Philadelphia, PA markets, become an Internal Auditor for the Northeastern Region at twenty-three years old and move to the corporate office as the Right Hand of the VP of Finance at twenty-six years old.

DANGEROUS DETOURS AND A DESTINED DELIVERANCE

Again, I thrived in the workplace, but I was on thin ice personally. I ruined the relationship with my first love. To mask the pain, I bought new clothes, went through multiple relationships, and went out many times throughout the week in the city of Atlanta. All of this to quiet the deafening silence of depression and frustration.

After being at home with the flu in May 1988, I was at my lowest. I did not want to work or talk to friends or family. In fact, I was contemplating how to end my life quietly. That day, my sister Zarita called—we have always been close—and she wanted to check on me. I was curt, disrespectful, and did not want to speak to her or anyone, so I hung up.

A couple of minutes later, Zarita's boyfriend called back and said, "Man, what is wrong with you? Your sister is crying, and she is worried about you!" I asked to speak with Zarita, and I apologized. God used Zarita to break up the plan I was making to end my life.

The next morning, after being away from church for over six years, I got up and went to worship at Greater Zion Hill Baptist Church on May 28, 1988. Senior Pastor Elijah Jones, Sr. was preaching, and when he extended the invitation to accept Jesus Christ as Savior and Lord, he used Matthew 6:33 (NASB) as his appeal:

"But seek first His kingdom and His righteousness, and all these things will be added to you."

As I stood up to walk down the aisle, I spoke to God, "Okay God, I hear You talking. Prove Yourself through my life and I will serve You the rest of my days." Thirty-six years later, He is still proving Himself through me despite my failures and faults. Thank You, Lord Jesus!

MANY YEARS LATER

After leaving the corporate retail roles, I enjoyed business success at the Manager, Director, Vice President, Senior Vice President, and C-Suite levels for major corporations in the financial technology payments business, leading and developing hundreds of employees across multiple sites! By the way, I went back to finish my Bachelor of Science degree in Management Communication and a Minor in Biblical Studies with magna cum laude honors in 2005—my mom was very happy!

In 1994, I accepted the call to preach the Gospel of Jesus Christ and have served as an Associate Minister, Assistant Pastor, Associate Pastor, and Elder in multiple churches, and Senior Pastor of a church plant (Abundant Life Community Church in Alpharetta, GA—we will talk about that later). Remember, my ultimate goal was to have my own lady's apparel and shoe store, and I was considering a dangerous detour to end my life. How did I get here, as a senior leader in corporate America, from being a college dropout and manager trainee of a retail store in Spartanburg, SC?

A CHILD-LIKE EXAMPLE OF GOAL PLANNING

How many parents out there had or have children who were (or still are) crazy about Legos? Our son, Myles, had an affinity and adverse relationship with Legos as a child. His eyes would light up when he saw the picture on the box, but his head would drop when he opened the box. Initially, he did not want to do the required detailed work, so he settled in on building the characters while I did the hard work!

You see, Myles had a desire for immediate gratification. I had the same challenge growing up as my big thing was model cars, but I would sometimes get frustrated reading through the directions because I just wanted to get to the end-product. As Myles got older, he took the initiative to start putting together age-appropriate Lego kits. As I got older, I got excited with the building process to get to the end-product.

Many of you may have had similar experiences. You want a Graduate degree, but once you start, you realize how hard it is to do and you stop. Some develop an Excel spreadsheet detailing how they will budget and get out of debt, but then have trouble executing and sticking to the plan. You are enamored with a new car, but once you get it, the monthly note and regular maintenance fill you with regret. Or maybe you see the plan to get into better overall health and shape and envision how you will look in new clothes, *but* you are struggling to stay on the required eating and exercising plan. (Ouch—I can identify with this one a lot!) If we are truthful, all of us have had at least one experience like I mentioned above. How does it happen?

I am grateful to God for the many gifts and talents He has bestowed upon me. I have been able to lead in the community, church, and within corporate America because of Him. The problem is, *if you are not careful, you can easily move forward in your talents and abilities and inadvertently leave God out.*

The funny thing is that you don't realize it until you are far down the road; crying out to God and asking Him, "Where are you, God?!"

The even funnier part is when the Holy Spirit reminds you that God is right where you left Him!

MOVING AHEAD OF GOD

An example of this is when I was the Senior Pastor of the church God planted through me. We had an opportunity to buy land early on, and, because I had the ability to provide the down payment, I did! What a huge mistake! My complete focus should have been on honoring God and developing the people who were connecting with us. Why was it wrong for me to jump in as an imposter Jehovah Jireh (God who provides)?

There are many reasons:

- ✍ The vision should have been bathed in more prayer and fasting.
- ✍ Those connecting with us should have had the opportunity to develop their faith and align it with where God was leading.
- ✍ This decision ended up hurting my family financially for years!

9

My motivation was right; to do it for the Kingdom of God, but the approach to accomplish the goal was all mine. God had not given me explicit directions. You see, if you are not careful, the very talents and abilities you have developed will tempt you to drive too fast and develop your own plans and leave God completely out. Once I realized what I had done, I begged God for forgiveness as I was out of order, and I had to face Leslie because it has impacted my family for over two decades.

REALIZE THAT GOD HAS A PLAN

Slow down—wait for what God wants! Jeremiah 29:11 (CSB) says, "For I know the plans I have for you—this is the Lord's declaration—plans for your well-being, not for disaster, to give you a future and a hope."

According to Google, this is the fourth most quoted Bible verse. I have used it to close sermons. I have used it as a core verse for a topical sermon. I have used it to encourage people who are in search of direction. But now, I have experienced the impact and application of this verse, within its context, multiple times in my personal life. Sharing the verse in a solely stand-alone context (vs.11 only) diminishes the power that God intends through the complete context.

The verse naturally drives us to ask several questions:

1. What kind of plans?
2. When will the plans happen?

3. How will I know they are God's plans?

4. What can I do to expedite experiencing these plans?

5. Do I need training to recognize these plans?

6. Is there a specific status I need to reach to ignite these plans?

7. Does God have steps to get us to discover His plans?

I am sure you can come up with many more questions. While they are legitimate questions if we are in control, they are impotent questions in the discovery of God's plans that are supernatural and are played out through God's providence and sovereignty in our relationship with Him.

A PRACTICAL VIEW OF DISCOVERING GOD'S PLAN

Here are the big ideas for this book:

We cannot use hope alone as a strategy for God to beam down blessings for us! If we walk with God, through our relationship with Jesus Christ, and want to discover His plans for us, we must participate and follow God's lead!

If we walk with God, through our relationship with Jesus Christ, and want to discover His plans for us, we must participate and follow God's lead!

This requires your participation—because *Some Assembly is Required!*

11

My goal is to teach you the two core actions you must take:

Prepare Practically

I hear you asking, "André, what does it mean to prepare practically?" As you journey through the coming chapters, you will see this played out in the lives of the children of Israel. They were in a less-than-optimal situation for a long period of time, but God showed them how to live above their circumstances.

Just as you prepare practically for multiple areas of your life every day, this story will show you that despite the pressures of life, we can walk in the power of our relationship with Jesus Christ in very practical ways. Don't allow the circumstances and situations of life to shackle you in bondage when God can show you how to break those chains and discover His plans for you!

Pursue Persistently

In life, relationships can grow from acquaintance to associate, from associate to friend, and from friend to best friend.

How? I am glad you asked that question! By simply pursuing a deeper level of intimacy with that person persistently.

Well, if we are to grow our relationships with others by a persistent pursuit, how much more should we be pursuing God persistently through our relationship with Jesus Christ? If we really want to discover God's plans for us, pursuing Jesus persistently must be our primary motive in every aspect of life.

This is not a *religious list* to follow, but rather it is a *relational way of life, with Jesus Christ.*

Are you ready to go on this journey with me? Let's go!

CHAPTER 1

STAY PRODUCTIVE AND MULTIPLY

*"Build houses and live in them. Plant
gardens and eat their produce."*

JEREMIAH 29:5 (CSB)

As I shared earlier, I have had great success as a Senior Executive Leader in the corporate environment, leading up to 800 employees across five sites. I have had roles such as Director, Vice President, Senior Vice President, Chief Service Officer, and Chief Operating Officer, but I have also had to adjust twice in my career to accept and operate in lesser roles. While the roles were important, they were not close to the Senior Executive Leader roles I had previously held. I was also impacted financially—for the first time in years, I was looking for a job (I had always previously been recruited) in January 2010, and I did not find a new role until May 2011.

Oh, did I mention the new role was paying me only about 45% of what I had previously made and that it required me to relocate my family two hours away?

This was quite disorienting at first—seeing my title, span of responsibility, influence, capability, and total compensation shrink was incredibly frustrating, but our country was in the midst of the Great Recession. I was grateful to land this role.

I had paradoxical feelings, though. On the one hand, I would have to leave the church God planted through me. It was like giving up a child. We made the two-hour commute for four months to keep leading the church.

While we were spiritually and emotionally in pain, God led us to a wonderful ministry in New Birth Outreach Center in Columbus, Georgia, where we were welcomed like family. Whether leading the couples ministry, preaching and teaching, or being the Worship Leader, this anointed ministry revived and renewed our souls.

Then I slowly started to realize that *I was sleeping through the class that God was teaching!* Because I was so focused on the detrimental parts of not having the former status and influence, I was missing the life-transforming lessons that could be learned through horizontal growth and by sitting at Jesus' feet as Mary did:

> As Jesus and His disciples were on their way, He came to a village where a woman named Martha opened her home to Him. She had a sister called Mary, who sat at the Lord's feet listening to what He said. But Martha was distracted by all the preparations that had to be made. She came to Him and asked, "Lord, don't You care that my sister has left me to do the work by

myself? Tell her to help me!" "Martha, Martha," the Lord answered, "you are worried and upset about many things, but few things are needed—or indeed only one. Mary has chosen what is better, and it will not be taken away from her." (Luke 10:38-42, NASB)

You see, Martha was focused on busy work (religious activity), while Mary was focused on learning from spending time with Jesus (relationship growth). When we spend time with Jesus, searching for His plans for us is revealed through developing a perpetually growing, intimate relationship with Him.

HORIZONTAL VS. VERTICAL GROWTH

Once I repented, I started sharing my knowledge and expertise with others, mentoring peers and other colleagues, volunteering for division-wide initiatives, and seeking out a mentor who wouldn't be easily impressed by my expertise and career success. I experienced this same path and growth within my walk as a Minister of the Gospel of Jesus Christ (from Associate Minister to Assistant Pastor, to Founding Senior Pastor, to Teacher, to Elder), and I am grateful to serve and be used by God at any level to glorify Him and to edify His people at Eagles Nest Church with my friend and Senior Pastor, Lee Allen Jenkins.

The choice is yours to make:

1. Live in bondage because you refuse to see what God is doing.

2. Change your mindset from, "God, why is this happening to me?" to "God, what do you want me to learn while I am here?"

By the way, I was promoted to a leadership role within my former company in April 2022 after seven tries of applying for other leadership goals within the same company! You cannot beat God's timing and plan! Effective January 2024, I serve as a Senior Director of Strategic Customer Success, leading nearly fifty wonderful employees at a SaaS technology company and leading a portfolio of approximately 450 customers and $300M in annual recurring revenue.

UNTAPPED POTENTIAL

You earned your degree. You put in the time. You have networked to make the right connections. You have done everything you know to do, and yet, you are still unfulfilled in your career.

It's simple: God's plans are always better than our plans, so we need to wait on Him.

Believing it must be the company, you decide to open yourself up to opportunities outside of the company. Now, the apparent "right" opportunity is in front of you—more money, more impressive title, hybrid work schedule—wow, this is awesome! You have found what you believe is God's plan for you.

Why then, after a short period of time, are you filled with regret? You have more money. You have the title. What's wrong? This feeling of despair is starting to drain the energy out of you daily, and now you are doing just enough to get by. Your aspirations of always being productive and multiplying your contribution are waning, and your attitude is lulling you into isolation and disengagement. What happened?

It is easy to fall into this type of trap when *we* orchestrate the plan rather than following God's sovereign and providential plan for us. But, if God has given us free will, why do we need to wait on His plans to develop?

It's simple: God's plans are *always* better than our plans, so we need to wait on Him. If you are not careful, you can easily strike out on your own. When you are educated and have certain expertise and experiences, you can subliminally start executing using your own ability. As you will see, the children of Israel had the same independent mindset.

GOD'S WAYS AND THOUGHTS

Before we start exploring this verse, we need to understand the context of Jeremiah 29:1-4. God had warned His people repeatedly about their disobedience and lack of consistent commitment to following Him (they had other plans too). He had also promised them that if they did not turn back to Him, He would allow their enemy to capture and exile them. But they did not listen or learn and now find themselves in a seventy-year exile under the Babylonian Empire. Many of us are likely nodding in the affirmative because we too have been in a place where we have gone against God's timing and His guidelines because we think we know best.

Now, the children of Israel are in captivity for seventy years, yet Almighty God enters the scene with a pronouncement of productivity and multiplication. This, of course, is not the first or only time that God makes declarations, commands, or gives directions we just don't understand. In Isaiah 55:8-9 (CSB) God states,

"For My thoughts are not your thoughts, and your ways are not My ways." This is the Lord's declaration. "For as heaven is higher than earth, so My ways are higher than your ways, and My thoughts than your thoughts."

Okay God, we get it, but doesn't it sound antithetical and nonsensical? Yes—when you look solely through your limited, natural eyes. This can truly be challenging because many of us are well-intentioned. We say to ourselves, "I have the education, expertise, and experience to develop and implement this plan...I will involve God in the things that are much larger or more complex!" When this approach doesn't work, we become disappointed and distant, and we begin to second guess ourselves, or, yes, we even blame God.

But when we choose to trust God to see situations, delays, denials, and disappointments through His perspective, we can shift from the predisposed desire of our will to trusting that His will is best for us.

COMPLACENCY OR CONTENTMENT?

If you are not careful, you can end up becoming bitter in bondage, leading to a mindset of *complacency*. Complacency is being self-satisfied, smug, or just disengaged where you are presently. It is like saying, "Well, I have always been in this environment," or, "No one is going to promote me or give me a chance," or, "That's okay. I'll do just enough to get by." Complacency can cause you to stop dreaming, to stop having aspirational goals, to stop pursuing, and to stop believing that God still has a plan.

The children of Israel could have easily fallen into a complacent mindset, but God comes to eradicate that thinking and He challenges them to move to *contentment*.

So, what does it mean to be content? It means a state of joy and satisfaction knowing that God has you where you are for a reason and a season. There was no way that the children of Israel were content to be under the captivity of the Babylonian Empire, but God challenged them to "Build houses and live in them. Plant gardens and eat their produce."

How do you find the strength, the courage, or the focus to live like you are free while in bondage? The answer is simple: finding contentment in your relationship with God, who providentially sent you into exile, will be the fuel that drives you to optimize where you are rather than becoming complacent and disengaged.

What if I stayed in the disconcerted mindset of no longer having the former status corporately, personally, financially, and ministerially? I would have drifted into complacency and would have eventually become bitter when God was using this version of *exile* to increase my effectiveness for Him. Don't allow the seemingly disheartening reality of a trial to cause you to become bitter or complacent! Turn to God, and He will show you what He wants to teach you in that season.

Oh, by the way, being content is not something we are born with. The Apostle Paul explains it this way in Philippians 4:11(NLT):

> "Not that I was ever in need, for I have learned how to be content with whatever I have."

GET TO WORK GOD'S WAY

In Jeremiah 29:5, God says, "Build houses and live in them. Plant gardens and eat their produce."

God, in essence, is telling them, "Although you are in bondage, I want you to live like you are free!" This was an agrarian culture, but the point is true in our modern-day, socio-economic environment: optimize where God has you now!

You may be asking, "How can I practically embrace these instructions today?"

Stop trying to make sense of God's instructions and simply yield to Him. Yielding to God's will creates a growing level of intimacy and trust in God through Jesus Christ.

Trust that if God allowed you to be where you are, there is a purpose. We will discuss this later, but learning to be content promotes greater dependence on God.

Accept that God is able to use your obedience even in the midst of adverse situations. Whether we created the adversity or not, our obedience to God in the midst of it sets the atmosphere for us to see Him move on our behalf.

BUILDING ON YOUR FAITH

Think about where you are in a few aspects of your life: the areas where you are not content and really want to understand God's plans. Are you staying productive and multiplying? If not, what can you do in those areas to position yourself to optimize where you are presently? What can God do through you with a new mindset?

The language in verse 5, from God to His people, speaks to positive activity. Based on what you learned in this chapter, how will you begin to live like you are free?

PRAYER

Heavenly Father, the tests, trials, and tragedies of this life can sometimes lull us into a spirit and mindset of complacency and bondage. If we allow it to linger, this mindset can make us bitter and delay our reconciliation with You. Let us find hope and the courage to optimize the state that we are in by knowing that You are with us, even when it is not in an optimal situation of our own making. Help us learn to be content, no matter what our circumstances are, and show us how to remain productive and multiply even when we appear to be in a dry season of life.

In Jesus' Name,
Amen!

CHAPTER 2

INCREASE YOUR INFLUENCE

"Find wives for yourselves and have sons and daughters. Find wives for your sons and give your daughters to men in marriage so that they may bear sons and daughters. Multiply there; do not decrease."

JEREMIAH 29:6 (CSB)

On August 1, 2000, I was named the first-ever Chief Service Officer. We were a publicly traded company with approximately 3,500 employees, and I managed almost a third of the employees. At that time, this was the pinnacle of success for my career—great salary, annual bonus, stock options, wonderful teams at each site! I reported to a great, very charismatic President and CEO and a great, very smart Founder and Chairman.

On the outside, I looked like an enviable success—my brand was impeccable in our company, with our clients, with my employees, and within the payments industry, *but on the inside, I was empty.*

My dad passed away when I was twenty-one, and, although I poured into the lives of my employees, company, and ministries, I was completely empty because no one had poured into me for decades. Don't get me wrong, Leslie and I were doing fine. I was generally okay, but I was completely empty on the inside. I was like, "God, I made it to the mountain top professionally, but why am I so empty?"

Finally, I reached out to one of God's most renowned Evangelists, Senior Pastors, Speakers, and Authors, Dr Crawford Loritts, and I asked him to become my mentor for the next several years. Thankfully, he agreed, and the knowledge and direction he imparted revived my soul. I was slowly being filled and was no longer empty as he pointed me to a greater level of intimacy with Jesus Christ.

THE DANGER OF TURNING INWARDLY

I was watching an NFL football game on Sunday and I witnessed how well one team was playing versus how poorly another team was playing. The team playing poorly not only struggled on the field; they struggled on the sidelines—arguing back and forth for the national TV audience to see. If we are not careful during life's pressures, we too can turn against ourselves and the people on our life team, rather than turning to God for His plans.

Even in difficulty, bondage, and when it seems there is no movement, we are to increase our influence.

Pressure can cause you to do this—the lack of understanding while waiting on God's plans to be revealed can cause you to do this. But God has another plan. Even in difficulty, bondage, and when it seems there is no movement, we are to *increase our influence*. Why did God want them to increase their influence? For His Glory and so that others are positively impacted for the Kingdom of God.

BE LIKE CHRIST AND LET HIM INCREASE YOUR INFLUENCE

In today's culture, you hear a lot about building your own brand. You see it across multiple social media platforms, and it is prevalent in the business and entertainment worlds as well. Build your brand, build your network, and become a power broker or power couple. There is nothing wrong with these things.

Well, except maybe the heavy focus on *you*.

Building your brand—socially and economically—is perfectly appropriate, especially in today's culture. But it is wise to ensure that there is an honorable, purpose-based foundation and motivation to support what you are building.

Why do you want to build your brand, and your network, or become a power broker or power couple? Who will be positively impacted by what you are building? Will God be glorified by the brand or network or your new influence level? Or will you take credit for all of the success?

Okay. This one may seem impossible at first thought, but I promise you that becoming Christ-centered will help you increase your influence for the Kingdom of God. The Apostle Paul captures a powerful example of what it takes to be like Jesus Christ:

> Therefore if there is any encouragement in Christ, if any consolation of love, if any fellowship of the Spirit, if any affection and compassion, ²make my joy complete by being of the same mind, maintaining the same love, united in spirit, intent on one purpose. ³Do nothing from selfishness or empty conceit, but with humility consider one another as more important than yourselves; ⁴do not merely look out for your own personal interests, but also for the interests of others. ⁵Have this attitude in yourselves which was also in Christ Jesus. (Philippians 2:1-5, NASB)

Wow! Think about this for a moment.

Paul is saying rather than increasing your influence using your natural talents and abilities, rather than looking for opportunities to build your brand, rather than seeking to be blessed in your pursuit of significance, why not try to increase your influence by being like Christ?

I have found that in my greatest times of need, and when I am seeking to become established or reach a certain goal, I can be overwhelmingly blessed by seeking to esteem others by helping them build their brand, and by encouraging and coaching them, rather than focusing on me.

Notice that Paul says three key phrases that relate to Increasing Your Influence:

- ✍ ³ Do nothing from selfishness or empty conceit, but with humility consider one another as more important than yourselves;

- ✍ ⁴ do not merely look out for your own personal interests, but also for the interests of others.

- ✍ ⁵ Have this attitude in yourselves which was also in Christ Jesus..."

Praise God! I am a witness that this does actually work.

Pouring into, encouraging, and serving others takes your mind off of your constant pursuit of building for you. It takes your mind off of why you haven't reached your goals yet. It literally centers you in someone else's life, and you get a chance to witness them come alive as they start to realize their goals and see their brand being built.

Here's the awesome part—God will see the sincerity of your heart and spirit, and He will reward you accordingly!

GOD'S CHALLENGE

In Chapter 1, I mentioned that in Jeremiah 29:5 (CSB), God instructed them to "Build houses and live in them. Plant gardens and eat their produce." This was essential to taking care of their primary needs, and He required their participation.

Now, God goes further in challenging His people—remember, they are in captivity under their enemies—in verse 6: "Find wives for yourselves and have sons and daughters. Find wives for your sons and give your daughters to men in marriage so that they may bear sons and daughters. Multiply there; do not decrease."

This is incredible! He not only wants their essential needs met in Jeremiah 29:5, but now God wants them to experience exponential increase!

EXPLORING JEREMIAH 29:6

There are three things we should take note of in this directive from God:

Increase Your Influence for the Present
This minimally impacts two generations: the adults at that time and the children that would come from their marriages.

Increase Your Influence for the Future
The parents above now become grandparents, and the children become parents.

Increase Your Influence Perpetually
Multiply there and do not decrease!

In the commentary of *The Tony Evans Study Bible*, Dr. Evans states, "God wanted His people to establish a kingdom presence in exile. While they were waiting for a better tomorrow, they were to be industrious today. Earth is not merely a place to wait for a ride to heaven. It's where we live out God's kingdom agenda in history."

Wow—what would happen on the Earth for the kingdom if every Christ-follower embraced and walked in this truth in every aspect of their lives?

When we find contentment in the fact that God has us where we are for a reason *and* a season, it should motivate us to increase our influence. I hear you asking, how do you do this? Let's look at the following examples.

The Workplace

As I said earlier, there is nothing wrong with desiring to move up vertically or horizontally and make the right connections with decision-makers at work or as an entrepreneur. But be careful—delays in getting an opportunity to be promoted or land a big deal can be handled as an opportunity to grow more in your role or business horizontally, or it can be handled as an opportunity to become bitter and disengaged as you wait for its manifestation.

To do the former, it really takes a concentrated effort to think:

- What skills can I sharpen?
- Is there a team member that I can help or mentor?
- Can I take on a stretch assignment or participate in a division-wide initiative?
- Who can I engage to be my mentor?
- Is there a class or a certification I can take to build my expertise?

    ᴥ How can I make sure my attitude and approach remain positive?

If you yield to and execute this mindset, God will certainly honor you and increase your influence within the workplace or your business.

Home

There are many things that can make your home environment feel like you're complacent or in a place of bondage or exile:

- ᴥ Sickness
- ᴥ Challenges with Children
- ᴥ Marital Issues
- ᴥ Financial Challenges
- ᴥ Unemployment
- ᴥ The Death of a Loved One
- ᴥ And many other items.

When these things arise, use the adversity as a teaching opportunity for your children and as a time to partner with your spouse to seek God together. Allow space for each of you to express how you are feeling without judgment. Listen to each other's ideas, questions, or recommendations.

Married couples, please do not turn on one another during the adversity, but rather, join forces and turn completely to God. If you are an unmarried adult, build and develop a small circle of accountability partners who can encourage, challenge, have fun with, or counsel you.

Approaching these varied situations with the mindset that "we need to seek God's plans to handle this" will certainly increase your influence within your home for generations to come. The beauty of this is that it will overflow into your workplace, your community, and your church—all because you decided to yield to God's plan where you are right now!

BUILDING ON YOUR FAITH

God gave the children of Israel very specific instructions on how to increase their influence. How can you take what He told them in Jeremiah 29:6 and apply it to your environment and the Kingdom of God?

Based on this chapter, how will you build your brand for God to influence the earth for Him?

PRAYER

Heavenly Father, we reject the tendency to turn inwardly and isolate ourselves when in storms or facing some type of adversity. When adversity impacts us directly, help us be aware that You have allowed the adversity, and there is something else in us that You want to bring out. Help us to understand that we can highlight Your glory and positively impact others by seeking to increase our influence under the guidance of the Holy Spirit. As we seek to connect horizontally, help us connect with others by being others-centric.

Help us to be like Christ.

In Jesus' Name,
Amen.

CHAPTER 3

CONTRIBUTE TO THE COMMUNITY

*"Pursue the well-being of the city I have
deported you to. Pray to the Lord on its
behalf, for when it thrives, you will thrive."*

JEREMIAH 29:7 (CSB)

The once pseudo-covert nature of divisiveness within our country was made much more visible through the political, racist, and socio-economic headlines of 2020–2022. It was literally heartbreaking to watch it play out in the midst of a global pandemic while a good portion of the Body of Christ remained silent.

I was particularly concerned because our son would be starting out on his own (during a global pandemic and with heightened racial tension) in college during the fall of 2020. Would his professors look at him as a student or as an African American student? How would police or others in authority see him upon their first look—as a student or as a suspect?

My goal had always been to raise a God-fearing, disciple of Jesus Christ who would continue to live for Him despite external pressures. Like all of us, he is imperfect, but he loves God and he loves his people.

I realized that we simply had to trust God.

The cry of the Prophet Habakkuk steadily rang loudly in my spirit:

> How long, Lord, must I call for help and You do not listen or cry out to You about violence, and You do not save? Why do You force me to look at injustice? Why do You tolerate wrongdoing? Oppression and violence are right in front of me. Strife is ongoing, and conflict escalates. Habakkuk 1:2-3 (CSB)

This short Minor Prophet book of the Bible captures the complete dialogue between Habakkuk and God, and it should give us hope for today. In the meantime, we have the video-based stain on the soul and consciousness of America that captured the murder of George Floyd on May 25, 2020, and there have been many others—too many to capture here.

While we have seen some justice recently, there have been unprecedented events as well, such as the January 6, 2021 riots on the Capitol and the recent killing of Sonya Massey. Please understand, I am not trying to politicize this book at all, but it is relevant to what I want to discuss in this chapter.

A CHRIST-LIKE RESPONSE IN THE MIDST OF ADVERSITY

The outcry against the senseless killings, and, in some cases, no justice for the victim, revealed a lot about the condition of our country's heart and consciousness. The polarization and prejudices really troubled me, especially how they became politicized and divisive. It caused me to reflect on the passage we often refer to as the Good Samaritan in Luke 10:30-37 (NASB):

> Jesus replied and said, "A man was going down from Jerusalem to Jericho, and he encountered robbers, and they stripped him and beat him, and went away leaving him half dead. And by coincidence a priest was going down on that road, and when he saw him, he passed by on the other side. Likewise a Levite also, when he came to the place and saw him, passed by on the other side. But a Samaritan who was on a journey came upon him; and when he saw him, he felt compassion, and came to him and bandaged up his wounds, pouring oil and wine on them; and he put him on his own animal, and brought him to an inn and took care of him. On the next day he took out two denarii and gave them to the innkeeper and said, 'Take care of him; and whatever more you spend, when I return, I will repay you.' Which of these three do you think proved to be a neighbor to the man who fell into the robbers' hands?" And he said, "The one who showed compassion to him." Then Jesus said to him, "Go and do the same."

The priest and the Levite in this parable represent the ritualistic religious people who worship together, live together, who see the trouble of this world, but yet choose not to really get engaged or contribute to the community. They would rather talk about how bad things are and politicize them rather than positively respond in any way. Or maybe, instead of intervening and helping, they would rather start recording and post what they saw on social media.

As Paul tells Timothy, people like this are "holding to a form of godliness although they have denied its power..." It is also important to call out their silence and inaction. The priest and Levite tried to bury their heads in the sand. As Christ followers, we must reject that type of approach. Life events can be messy, uncomfortable, painful, and sensitive, but that doesn't excuse us from getting involved and starting to positively contribute to the community.

But then, the socially and culturally despised and rejected Samaritan comes along, and he is immediately moved with compassion. The Samaritan doesn't call a meeting about it, nor does he post on Facebook, X, or Instagram. Instead, human compassion drives him to do what the "religious people" refused to do—contribute to the community. This Samaritan not only rendered immediate care and assistance, but he also provided transportation, lodging, and finances.

But those tangible things weren't actually the main point! The most important thing was his decision to invest himself relationally—just like Jesus Christ does for us.

Jesus clearly calls out that the Samaritan was the true neighbor to this wounded person. We too can be a good neighbor, even in highly sensitive or volatile times, by simply doing one thing under the power of the Holy Spirit. Contribute to the community as Jesus demonstrates in this parable. Don't allow what some think are inconveniences to keep you from engaging and getting involved in the lives of God's people.

Don't allow what some think are inconveniences to keep you from engaging and getting involved in the lives of God's people.

A NOTE TO SENIOR AND LEAD PASTORS

If we are ever to effectively challenge the children of God to pursue unity and to speak out against injustices, our church leadership must echo the same from the foundational truths of God's Word. Pastors must reject allowing the church to become a platform for projecting cultural and political biases that eat away at the foundational principles of the Gospel of Jesus Christ.

Speaking out does not have to be loud and have a "red meat" approach. It can be taught to the believer and seeker alike through the teachings of Jesus Christ. Be committed to Jeremiah 29:7 and pursue the good for our country, this world, and all of its people—especially in times of adversity and injustice, for when you do, the church will overtly impact multiple aspects of our culture.

CONTRIBUTE TO THE COMMUNITY GOD'S WAY

Jeremiah 29:7 could not be any clearer. God has told them how to stay productive and multiply in Jeremiah 29:5 to meet their essential needs. He then tells them to increase their influence in Jeremiah 29:6 to promote exponential growth and service. Now, God tells them to contribute to the community in Jeremiah 29:7:

> "Pursue the well-being of the city I have deported you to.
>
> Pray to the Lord on its behalf, for when it thrives, you will thrive."

God, in essence, is saying you're in bondage, but:

- Live like you are free.
- Multiply and do not decrease.
- Be people of character and not corruption.

I can somewhat understand (but do not accept) the divisiveness in the community and the culture, but how does the Church allow itself to become a replica of the divisiveness in our country? As a part of the Body of Christ, our individual and collective goals must be to:

Pursue the Well-being of Others
We should not strive for *uniformity* or sameness, but rather, we should strive for *unity* or togetherness. Human beings will have differences. That is expected. However, we should unite around the core principles of the Bible, regardless of our race, personal preferences, socio-economic status,

political affiliation, or beliefs. This also means that we should resume our position of influencing the culture rather than the culture overtly influencing and driving the church.

PRAY TO THE LORD ON OUR WORLD'S BEHALF

As stated earlier, the events of 2020-2022 and beyond should have those who believe in the power of prayer in a posture of prayer daily. Senseless killings, a global pandemic and its impacts, a shaky and sometimes corrupt political system, a volatile economy, and a new wave of employment challenges are more than enough to keep us in a perpetual position of prayer for our country and our world. 2 Chronicles 7:14 (NKJV) gives us a great picture of how God can intervene when His people lean into God through prayer rather than through politics:

> If My people who are called by My name will humble themselves, and pray and seek My face, and turn from their wicked ways, then I will hear from heaven, and will forgive their sin and heal their land.

WHEN IT THRIVES, YOU WILL THRIVE

We should be actively engaged in politics, business, social causes, justice, economic development, helping the impoverished, etc. These are things God required then, and He expects them of us now! But we must be careful not to be dragged into the divisiveness that is in the culture and politics. When we pursue the well-being of our community, verse 7 says that it will thrive and so will we.

BUILDING ON YOUR FAITH

God gave the children of Israel a very clear path to follow on behalf of the city: pursue its well-being and pray on its behalf.

Meditate on verse 7 for a moment.

- ∽ What is God saying to you about opportunities to seek the well-being of others and to pray on behalf of your community, church, corporation, business, or family?

- ∽ How will they benefit from your persistent contribution?

- ∽ How will you benefit from taking this approach?

Based on this chapter, how can God use your contribution to your community?

PRAYER

Heavenly Father, Your words are very clear in Jeremiah 29:7. Help us show the world what this verse will do to the earth when Christ followers reject personal, prejudicial, and political preferences and pick up Your purpose and carry out Your plan. Help us use Your word to drive our actions so that we can appropriately contribute to the community. Thank You, Father!

In Jesus' Name,
Amen.

CHAPTER 4

BLOCK THE HATERS

*"For this is what the Lord of Armies, the
God of Israel says, 'Don't let your diviners
deceive you, and don't listen to the dreams
you elicit from them. For they are prophesying
falsely to you in My name. I have not sent
them.' This is the Lord's declaration."*

JEREMIAH 29:8, 9 (CSB)

I still remember the teasing I would get from some of my classmates after graduating high school. A lot were working in the booming textile or manufacturing industries in South Carolina, while I was managing a ladies' and children's shoe and apparel store. Other classmates went to college while I dropped out to work full-time to help my family. I remember my mom telling me how one of my best friend's dad rebuked her for "letting me" drop out of college to work. He meant well, but he was completely out of line.

Neither group of former classmates knew that God had plans for me—from running one store to becoming Regional Internal Auditor over approximately 150 stores in the Northeast. From starting as a supervisor in the financial technology industry to becoming the Chief Service Officer for a 3,500-employee company eleven years later. From opening and closing the nightclubs in Atlanta to becoming a Minister of the Gospel and a Senior Pastor of a church.

I went from being a college dropout to becoming a college graduate with Magna cum Laude honors twenty-five years later!

As Jeremiah tells them, "Don't let your diviners deceive you, and don't listen to the dreams you elicit from them. For they are prophesying falsely to you in My name. I have not sent them."

God can do anything He wants to do, through anyone He chooses to do it! Hallelujah!

HATERS ARE NOT NEW

The term "haters" became popular in the 1990s largely through the colorful stories told by hip-hop artists through their music. Terms like *"Haters Gonna Hate"* and *"Playa Haters"* leaped from the lyrics and beats of hip-hop to pop culture, and they are still used today. The sentiment here is that the criticism used is more reflective of the state of the critic or hater (their insecurities) rather than the one being criticized.

While it is unfortunate, be aware of the fact that you will have haters! Below are some of their characteristics:

- ∽ Haters will always want to know more about your life and plans than they will reveal about their own.

- ∽ When you reveal your plans, goals, or accomplishments, haters will try to "one up" whatever you reveal.

- ∽ Haters will want updates to see if you are tracking towards your goals so they can stand in judgment of your progress or lack of progress.

- ∽ Haters seem confident externally, but often their foundational actions are based on their insecurities.

- ∽ Haters can be influential and cause you to second guess waiting on God to reveal His plans for you.

While this terminology took root in the 1990s and still exists today, haters are not new! In fact, the Bible is replete with examples of God's people and the haters they had to deal with:

Moses

The Hebrew-born Egyptian prince became a shepherd in exile after murdering an Egyptian soldier. Then, God called Moses to become the servant leader He would use to speak to Pharoah and lead the children of Israel through the Red Sea and the wilderness en route to the promised land.

After they had an incredible time of worship and praise after crossing the Red Sea in Exodus 15, they soon complained of thirst in Exodus 15:22-27. Though the water was bitter, God gave them a tree to put it in to make it sweet.

Once they were no longer thirsty, they complained about being hungry in Exodus 16, but God gave them a daily allotment of manna to eat. Then in Exodus 16:9-13, Moses now must address their complaints about having no meat.

> Then Moses told Aaron, "Say to the entire Israelite community, 'Come before the LORD, for he has heard your grumbling.'" While Aaron was speaking to the whole Israelite community, they looked toward the desert, and there was the glory of the LORD appearing in the cloud. The LORD said to Moses, "I have heard the grumbling of the Israelites. Tell them, 'At twilight you will eat meat, and in the morning you will be filled with bread. Then you will know that I am the LORD your God.'" That evening quail came and covered the camp, and in the morning there was a layer of dew around the camp. Exodus 16:9-13 (NIV)

This had to be exhausting to Moses and infuriating to God. The very people Moses was called to lead out of bondage in God's power became Moses' haters multiple times in the wilderness.

KING DAVID

Can you imagine having to flee from your own son? King David finds himself in this situation in Psalm 3:1-3 as he was on the run from his son Absalom:

Lord, how my foes increase! There are many who attack me. Many say about me, "There is no help for him in God." But You, Lord, are a shield around me, my glory, and the one who lifts my head. Psalm 3:1-3 (CSB)

King David was in a world of trouble; some due to his own sin! But don't miss the most important point—although this was a serious issue, and he was indeed in trouble, *King David's focus is really on his relationship with God.* If the truth is told, many of us are the antithesis of this, and we get distracted by the pressure and the attacks from the haters and sometimes view God as a last option.

DON'T LET HATERS BLOCK GOD'S PLANS FOR YOU

Now, let's spend some time learning about the haters in Jeremiah 29:8-9.

For this is what the Lord of Armies, the God of Israel says, "Don't let your diviners deceive you, and don't listen to the dreams you elicit from them. For they are prophesying falsely to you in My name. I have not sent them." This is the Lord's declaration. Jeremiah 29:8-9 (CSB)

God is our source of counsel, and He has provided the Holy Spirit as our constant companion for guidance, teaching, comfort, conviction, and repentance. We should also have a small team that can be counted on here on Earth, who can listen to, pray with, and encourage us in line with God's Word and plans. If you are married, your wife or husband should absolutely be part of that team along with other trusted advisors. *But God gives us the ultimate counsel about His plans.*

As is the pattern in the Bible, God had warned His people multiple times against listening to the very people listed in Jeremiah 29:8-9. Below are a few examples:

> But the Lord said to me, "These prophets are prophesying a lie in My name. I did not send them, nor did I command them or speak to them. They are prophesying a false vision, worthless divination, the deceit of their own minds. Jeremiah 14:14 (CSB)

> So, you should not listen to your prophets, diviners, dreamers, fortune-tellers, or sorcerers who say to you, 'Don't serve the king of Babylon!' They are prophesying a lie to you so that you will be removed from your land. I will banish you and you will perish.
> Jeremiah 27:9-10 (CSB)

> Do not listen to the words of prophets who are telling you, 'Don't serve the king of Babylon, for they are prophesying a lie to you. I have not sent them – this is the Lord's declaration – and they are prophesying falsely in My name: therefore, I will banish you, and you will perish – you and the prophets who are prophesying to you.
> Jeremiah 27:14-15 (CSB)

You see, in Biblical days and now, haters had and still have no Godly plans. Their only goal is to distract you from reaching your divine destination. Many times, it is not deliberate, as their motivation could be lessening you to make themselves feel better by covering up their insecurities. You can mitigate their power by staying focused on pursuing the plans that God has for your life through Jesus Christ. Don't let haters distract you!

GOD KNOWS YOUR ADDRESS

I understand—it is tempting to allow others to speak into you while you are waiting to discover God's plans. This lack of patience, or inability to hear and to allow God to speak and reveal His plans, could easily drive you to make the wrong decisions. (Remember my decision to pay the down payment on land when I was the Senior Pastor of the church plant?)

Remember, the people saying, *"God said"* are many times well-intentioned. However, they are many times *not* speaking for God. God has your address, and He will reach you in the proper season. Galatians 6:9 says, "Let us not get tired of doing good, for we will reap at the proper time if we don't give up."

God has your address, and He will reach you in the proper season. If you are confused about what God is going to do or feel complacent where you are, there is a simple, God-honoring way to be content with a laser-like focus to honor God and reject haters. *Continue doing* *the things that God revealed to you the last time He spoke until He reveals His new plans for you. This will give Him the glory He is due, and it will edify the people who witness and hear your journey.*

And guess who will be in check? You guessed it—the haters!

A CALL FOR HEAVENLY INTERVENTION AGAINST HATERS

Whether on social media, in the workplace, or in other face-to-face engagements, haters want to block you at every turn. They are scheming, judgmental, and they desire to tear you down while building themselves up. King David cries out to God for heavenly intervention against haters in Psalm 109:1-3 (NIV):

> My God, whom I praise, do not remain silent, for people who are wicked and deceitful have opened their mouths against me; they have spoken against me with lying tongues. With words of hatred they surround me; they attack me without cause.

Our children face tremendous pressure against bullies—haters in our contemporary culture. Parents, we must be on guard against this type of engagement in the lives of our children. These unwarranted attacks not only eat away at the self-esteem of our children, but they also lead others tragically to suicide. Please request help from your school's administration and teachers, counselors, and church leaders.

This is also a teaching moment with our children. Resist the urge to preach or respond in a panicked way, but rather, get them to open up by being transparent and vulnerable while you listen empathetically.

If required, get them the counseling they need to overcome these attacks. Always remind them of God's plans for them and that blocking haters is a part of the journey. Teach them to replace the voice of haters with the destiny-centered voice of our Savior and Lord, Jesus Christ! Lastly, encourage them with this word from God in 1 John 4:4 (NIV):

> You, dear children, are from God and have overcome them, because the one who is in you is greater than the one who is in the world.

Unmarried adults, resist the temptation that haters will try to interject in your lives as well. Don't be surprised when they try to normalize what you know to be wrong in God's eyes just so you won't be lonely or alone.

Remember, haters are anyone who wants to derail you from your God-centered destiny by encouraging you to satisfy your soul's desires rather than yielding your spirit to the leading of the Holy Spirit. And, just in case there are some unmarried haters reading this book, I have a couple of verses for you in 1 Corinthians 6:19-20 (NIV):

> Do you not know that your bodies are temples of the Holy Spirit, who is in you, whom you have received from God? You are not your own; you were bought at a price. Therefore, honor God with your bodies.

Married adults, haters are also those who want to give you guidance in your marriage when theirs is already derailed. Reject the "Well, if I were you, I would..." advice because you will do further damage to your relationship. Instead, get connected to a solid, Christian-based marriage counselor to receive healing in your marital relationship.

Just in case there are some *"Well, if I were you..."* married haters reading this book, stay out of others' marital problems and follow this guidance from God's Word in Ephesians 5:33 (NIV):

> However, each one of you also must love his wife as he loves himself, and the wife must respect her husband.

In your workplace and business, haters may question why you are trying to work and lead with integrity when you can take shortcuts like they did to become successful quickly. Those haters will tell you, "Everyone does it...," "No one will know...," or, "It's okay to compromise your character..."

Just in case there are some career haters reading this book, I have a couple of verses that will help you understand why we will not compromise from Colossians 3:23, 24 (NKJV):

> And whatever you do, do it heartily, as to the Lord and not to men, knowing that from the Lord you will receive the reward of the inheritance; for you serve the Lord Christ.

LIFE APPLICATION TO HELP YOU BLOCK HATERS

Do not listen to them.

This is common throughout our core passage and the others I shared from Jeremiah. When we are waiting for God's plans to be revealed, we cannot give in to the temptation to listen to people God has not shared our plans with.

Run when people start a sentence with, *"Well, if I were you, I would..."* Politely remind them that you are not them and they are not you (and share your best smile). The sovereign God of the universe knows who you are and where you are, so He doesn't have to look for you to reveal His plans.

Do not be fooled by those with God-related titles.

God specifically calls out the prophets who are declaring, *"Thus says the Lord!"* This type of person can be obvious but sometimes they are a little subtle; at least to start.

Before long, the alleged prophecy becomes more of a personal preference or perspective that does not align with what God said. The more you pursue intimacy with Jesus Christ, the closer you are to God revealing His plans to you.

Remember what God said.

Yes! God can use others to confirm and affirm what He has been sharing, but you will know when it is God using someone to exhort and encourage you in what He has already spoken to you.

Stand on God's Word and the revelation of His plans for you.

BUILDING ON YOUR FAITH

Okay, it is time to be *really* transparent here:

- When have you allowed haters to speak into your life while waiting for God's plans to be revealed?

- What would you do differently to prevent a recurrence?

Now that you have completed this chapter, what can you do, in partnership with the Holy Spirit, to recognize and block the haters from the enemy?

PRAYER

Heavenly Father, thank You for clearly calling out the people who are opposing You. Help us be more diligent and focused on what You have said rather than on the perspectives of others. Let us be cognizant of the fact that the enemy of our soul will use haters to distract us from discovering the plans You have for us. We want to reach the divine destiny that You have in store! Please have the Holy Spirit convict and correct us when we are drifting from You to the opinions of others.

In Jesus' Name,
Amen.

PREPARE PRACTICALLY

I n Chapter 1, I shared that the children of Israel were in exile under their enemies, the Babylonians, for seventy years. Because of their lack **Make sure you understand whose** of faith in and reverence for **plan it is throughout your journey.** God, He used their enemy to rule and reign over them.

Then God gave them instructions on how to live free while in bondage, or to prepare practically for the plans of God to be revealed:

- ∾ Stay productive and multiply in verse 5.
- ∾ Increase your influence in verse 6.
- ∾ Contribute to the community in verse 7.
- ∾ Block the haters in verses 8, 9.

As we close out Part 1, I want to share a few passages with you that may help you have the right mindset and spirit when it feels like you are seemingly in bondage or exile:

Whose Plan Is It Anyway?

Make sure you understand whose plan it is throughout your journey. We can easily convince ourselves that we are rightly motivated and prepared but end up missing what God wants for us because we leave Him out. Internalize this passage and apply it to your activities, no matter the environment, and God will be honored.

> The reflection of the heart belongs to mankind, but the answer of the tongue is from the Lord. All a person's ways seem right to him, but the Lord weighs the motives. Commit your activities to the Lord, and your plans will be established. Proverbs 16:1-3 (CSB)

Learn to Be Satisfied Where God Has You

As I shared earlier, we want to stay away from complacency when preparing to receive God's plans. Contentment means to be satisfied, or to have an interdependent sufficiency that says, "God has me here for a reason and a season, so I will submit to what He wants me to learn until He is ready to move me!" This is *huge*—please don't overlook this perspective!

> But godliness with contentment is great gain. 1 Timothy 6:6 (CSB)

Remember Who You REALLY Work For

Man, did I ever have to learn this lesson! When I joined the financial technology industry, I enjoyed ten years with a retail corporation, receiving multiple promotions and recognition at the store, regional, and corporate office levels. Although I was making great progress in the financial technology industry, I had only been promoted once in the first eighteen months.

I know, I was a super aggressive, but successful, up-and-comer with *no patience*. I was also only two years into my relationship with Jesus Christ. One day, after a bout with the Senior Executive team (I almost got fired), the Holy Spirit convicted me strongly. God was not happy with me, nor was I happy, because I did not represent Him well. Remember, building your brand and network to expand your career or business horizontally and vertically is cool, but honor Jesus Christ as your Manager and Mentor so you won't leave Him out.

> Whatever you do, do it from the heart, as something done for the Lord and not for people, knowing that you will receive the reward of an inheritance from the Lord. You serve the Lord Christ. Colossians 3:23, 24 (CSB)

I hope Part 1 has blessed you.

Now, let's get ready for Part 2: *Pursue Persistently.*

PART TWO

Discovering God's Plans Requires You to Pursue Persistently

JEREMIAH 29:10-14

WHAT DOES IT MEAN TO PURSUE SOMETHING?

In actor Will Smith's *The Pursuit of Happyness*, there is a scene where his character, Christopher Gardner, finishes playing basketball with his son. He is encouraging his son to pursue his goals and dreams no matter the obstacles:

> Christopher Gardner: *"Hey. Don't ever let somebody tell you...You can't do something. Not even me."*
>
> Christopher (son): *"Alright."*
>
> Christopher Gardner: *"You gotta dream...You gotta protect it. People can't do something themselves, they wanna tell you you can't do it."*

This exchange speaks to the tenacity we must have in life to pursue our dreams and our goals. This pursuit must also be supported by what we talked about in Part 1: *Prepare Practically.*

For instance, someone who has a dream of being a medical doctor cannot enter medical school without preparing practically through the required undergraduate studies. Someone aspiring to be drafted into the NFL, NBA, MLB, MLS, or NHL can't pursue that dream without first preparing practically through the development of their athletic talents.

A dream of being a lawyer will fail if there is no practical preparation to qualify for law school before trying to gain admission. A dream of becoming a successful entrepreneur will fail miserably if you have not developed a business plan, secured financing, properly advertised and marketed, or made the appropriate connections for merchandise and shipping.

WHO OR WHAT ARE WE PURSUING?

But when I say we must *pursue persistently,* it is wise to ask, "What are you talking about?" If we are to discover God's plans for us, we must pursue *God* persistently! Not for stuff but for Him!

Do you look at your relationship with Jesus Christ as "Blessed *Insurance*" or "Blessed *Assurance*?" Another way of saying this is, "Do you persistently pursue Jesus for *what He can provide*, or do you pursue Jesus because of *who He is*?"

Do you look at your relationship with Jesus Christ as "Blessed Insurance" or "Blessed Assurance?"

One of the challenges with pursuing God only through a primary lens of religious academia is that you will get to know *about* God only. But when we *pursue God relationally* through the acceptance of Jesus Christ as Savior and Lord, we are more focused on *His Person* rather than *His Possessions.* Christ followers must also guard against this temptation.

Don't get me wrong...I am sure all of us, at one time or another, were pursuing the thing we were asking God for more than persistently pursuing Him in that situation. I hear you asking, "André, how do I guard against falling into this mode of seeking *stuff,* rather than seeking *the Savior?*" I am so glad that you asked that question! Proverbs 3:5, 6 (NLT) gives us the way to stay grounded and/or re-center ourselves:

"Trust in the LORD with all your heart, do not depend on your own understanding. Seek His will in all you do and He will show you which path to take."

In Jeremiah 29:10-14, we will see God's message to the children of Israel that He must be pursued persistently—not just when we are in trouble or in need or for our dreams to be manifested—but *always.*

Strap in! Chapters 5–9 will really show us how to become more intimate with God and how to position ourselves to receive His plans for us.

CHAPTER 5

REMEMBER THAT GOD CARES

For this is what the Lord says; "When seventy years for Babylon are complete, I will attend to you and will confirm My promise concerning you to restore you to this place."

JEREMIAH 29:10 (CSB)

"God, where are You?!"

That question is one of fear and uncertainty. Every believer and even some unbelievers have likely uttered those very words before.

Leslie and I certainly have.

After seven years of trying to conceive a child and being told that we could not, we learned on Christmas Eve of 1997 that Leslie was pregnant! *What a gift!* We shared the news with family and friends who had been in constant prayer for us, and everyone was excited.

We were excited about going to our second obstetrician's visit in mid-February of 1998 and wanted to hear the heart beating again on the ultrasound. Finally, the doctor came in and started asking questions as her assistant prepared Leslie for the ultrasound examination.

We could see the picture of our little girl, but there was no heartbeat.

It seemed like the blood drained from our faces, and I felt like screaming right there in the examination room. Our doctor finally confirmed that our little girl had passed.

I was in the middle of accepting a new senior leadership role in Delaware, and that ride to the temporary housing seemed to last forever. After trying to console Leslie and myself, I cried out in my spirit, *"God! Where are You?!"*

We were blessed, through a senior executive level offer, to relocate to Atlanta in March of 1998, and, in October of 1998, we learned that we were expecting again! All the doctor's visits were going well. Leslie was resting and taking great care of herself and our unborn daughter, and I was hovering like a male lion over his pride. In mid-February of 1999, I went to get some great soul food after church from The Beautiful in Southwest Atlanta when I received a frantic call from Leslie—she was bleeding and afraid.

I hurried home and rushed her to South Fulton Hospital. One week earlier, we had gone to our OB doctor to complain about what seemed to be contractions, and they had given Leslie a prescription to slow down that activity. Unfortunately, the amniotic fluid was leaking on that dreadful Sunday, and the dilation process had started.

Leslie lay inverted in the bed for several days doing everything a mother could do to save Faith Elizabeth Blythe, but the heartbeat slowly started to dissipate. She was only five months in the womb. We lost our second little girl within twelve months of losing our first.

Leslie and I were in anguish. Our church family, Elizabeth Baptist Church, and friends and family tried to comfort us, but it did no good. Additionally, Leslie lost a lot of blood during surgery and had to have four transfusions. I was afraid that I would lose her, too. I cried out again, *"God! Where are You?!"*

I have to be honest with you...I was angry with God.

While I had been a Christ follower for eleven years and a minister of the Gospel of Jesus Christ for four and a half years, I was angry. It was as if my anger had exiled me or built a wall between God's presence and me.

I did not want to hear anything about faith, prayer, scripture, belief, or *anything!* I could not pray. I could only cry and wail in private. I put the faith face on in front of Leslie, but frankly, I was hurting so bad for her, that I lost focus on my own healing and became functionally depressed.

I even stayed away from church, and I kept crying out, *"God! Where are You?!"* Even now, as I write about this, I am tearing up remembering my two daughters.

GOD'S UNIQUE WAY OF ANSWERING MY QUESTION

My late mom, Jessie, Leslie's late mom, Corlee, her stepdad, Lloyd, and many other family and friends had been there to support us at the hospital and at home afterward. But now we were alone. All I could do was hold her and remind her of my love for her, but, secretly, I was falling apart as well.

Then God answered as only He can. I was volunteering my service as an Associate Minister at Elizabeth Baptist Church, under Bishop Dr. Craig L. Oliver, Sr., and I received a call. A couple at the church who I knew had just delivered their child stillborn. The staff at church asked me if I could leave my office to go minister to this couple at Northside Hospital in Atlanta. I was a Vice President at a bank in Buckhead, so I was close by.

Why was God putting me in this place?

I was still healing myself from the loss of two baby girls within twelve months! My thoughts shifted from, "*God, where are You?*" to, "*God, what are You doing?!*"

Oddly enough, I did not hesitate to go, but I did not include Leslie. When I arrived, the parents were devastated. I tried to console them, and they asked me to hold and pray over their lifeless child. Through God's power, I garnered the strength to minister to them in the midst of this painful loss and my own unhealed pain.

God wasn't through.

Within five months of losing our last pregnancy, Leslie accompanied me on another visit to the hospital to minister to a couple who had lost a pregnancy. Through all of this, I found and embraced Psalm 139. King David describes God's attributes as omniscient—all-knowing, omnipresent—ever present, and omnipotent—all-powerful.

I wrote a sermon that personally ministered me back to healing and health called, *"Father Knows Best."* Additionally, God did what only He can by blessing us with the birth of our son, Myles, who, at the time of this writing, is twenty-two years old! He is a beautiful young man who has a heart and soul for the things of God and His people, and we are so blessed and honored to have him as our son!

AN INTROSPECTIVE LOOK

All of us have likely had at least one *"God, where are You?!"* or a *"God, do You really care?!"* moment. It could have come as a result of a failed business or the loss of a job. Maybe it showed up as turmoil in your marriage or anxiety related to raising your children.

One of the stumbling blocks that impede our progress in these moments is our unwillingness to be honest with God. We carry on in a religious, ritualistic, and routine way as if the omniscient (all-knowing) God of the Universe doesn't already know what you are feeling and thinking. But King David cries out in his intimate relationship with God in

Psalm 139:1-6 (NIV) to acknowledge that it is better to open up to God, even in our pain:

> You have searched me, LORD, and You know me. You know when I sit and when I rise; You perceive my thoughts from afar. You discern my going out and my lying down; You are familiar with all my ways. Before a word is on my tongue You, LORD, know it completely. You hem me in behind and before, and You lay Your hand upon me. Such knowledge is too wonderful for me, too lofty for me to attain.

Just like your car cannot move forward with any sustained power while in neutral, neither can you until you come face-to-face relationally with your Father in these types of moments. Tell God how you are feeling. Tell God how you are hurting. But then, move forward in trust, knowing that God still cares.

Tell God how you are feeling. Tell God how you are hurting. But then, move forward in trust, knowing that God still cares.

Many have shared with me that they are immobilized by disappointing God and believe those negative feelings disqualify them from God revealing His plans.

Believe me...God still cares!

Not only does God care, but King David also says that He already knows how we are feeling. I don't know about you, but for me, Psalm 139:4 really sums up just how much God really cares for us:

Before a word is on my tongue You, LORD, know it completely.

In other words, the only ones we are fooling when we do not open up to God are ourselves and other people. God wants you to open up! Our willingness to open up to God shows a dependence on and trust in God to bring us through. God's plan for Leslie and me to become parents still came to pass even though we experienced great loss before discovering those plans. Keep trusting and believing that His plans for you will come to pass.

LOOKING AT JEREMIAH 29:10

So, what does all that have to do with Jeremiah 29:10? In verses 5-9, God had encouraged His people in what may have been a strange way to them. He told them to:

- Stay productive and multiply – vs.5.
- Increase your influence – vs.6.
- Contribute to the community – vs.7.
- Block the haters – vs.8, 9.

Even though they were held captive under their enemies, the Babylonians, God encouraged them to live like they were free. In verse 10, God encouraged them to *remember that He cares.*

Let's break it down to find out how this can be applied to us:

"When seventy years for Babylon are complete."

The first thing that jumps out to me is the fact that God says that they will complete the seventy-year exile period. This means that some of them hearing God's declaration would possibly no longer be alive when the seventy years for Babylon are complete.

Wait a minute, God...didn't You just encourage us in verses 5-9 to live like we are free in the midst of exile?

Yes, God encouraged them. He wants them to know that He still cares and that they will still have to complete the period of exile. This is a reminder that while God does forgive us of sin through our relationship with Jesus Christ, there are still consequences to disobedience. Don't allow disobedience to distract you from discovering the plans God has for your life.

In Galatians 6:7 (NIV) the Apostle Paul states,

> Do not be deceived: God cannot be mocked. A man reaps what he sows.

"I will attend to you and will confirm My promise concerning you." God states, "I still care, and I have not forgotten My promise concerning you." He is faithfully attentive to His people while they are in exile and facing adversity (vs.5-9), but He has something greater in store once the seventy years are over.

The great news is that they would experience His goodness even while in exile. This should really encourage us! If God said it, the promise will come to pass! God uses His all-wise providence to fulfil His promises.

"To restore you to this place."

If we are faithful, even during times of exile or in storms, God has an expected end for us. I love that He speaks to us like a parent. "You impacted our relationship by acting like someone else's child and as a result, there is correction. Although you are under correction, you are still my son or daughter! I want you to begin doing good while under my correction, and I will in turn fully restore you after it is over."

Wow. What a good, good Father we have!

The Reiteration of God's Promise

Another way to remember that God cares, while trying to discover His plans for us, is to understand that when He makes a promise, God will repeat the promise. Jeremiah 29:10 is a reiteration of what God had already promised in Jeremiah 25:12 (CSB):

> When the seventy years are completed, I will punish the King of Babylon and that nation—this is the Lord's declaration—the land of the Chaldeans, for their iniquity and I will make it a ruin forever.

While, at times, it may seem that God has forgotten or that He is delayed, *remember that God cares!*

BUILDING ON YOUR FAITH

Based on my testimony and God's promise in Jeremiah 29:10, can you now look back on something God allowed that made you question His care for you?

   ❧ If yes, how do you look at that experience now?

   ❧ If not, understand that just because God allows things to happen through His all-wise sovereignty and providence, it doesn't mean that He does not care.

Based on what is shared in this chapter, do you now feel better prepared to remember God cares? How does Psalm 139:4 encourage you to open up more to our heavenly Father?

PRAYER

Heavenly Father, sometimes the storms of life are so challenging that we, while in pain and despair, question Your care for us. Please forgive us and reassure us that despite how things look, You still love us and care for us and will restore us. We pray that during difficult and uncertain times, the Holy Spirit will comfort us and remind us of Your promises to us so we do not fall into depression or give in to distractions. Help us, Father, to perpetually pursue intimacy with you so that we are reassured of Your presence, power, and protection. Show us what you want us to learn in the midst of the storm, and we will hold on to Your promises.

In Jesus' Name,
AMEN!!!

CHAPTER 6

RECOGNIZE THAT GOD'S PROMISES ARE TRUE

"For I know the plans I have for you—this is the Lord's declaration—plans for your well-being, not for disaster, to give you a future and a hope."

JEREMIAH 29:11 (CSB)

For years as a child, I was afraid of large dogs. In fact, if I saw that "Beware of Dog" sign in someone's yard, I would move quickly to the other side of the street. Many times, the dogs were chained to a pole or behind a fence, but the mere sight of them and the sound of their bark really unsettled me as I was on the way to my destination. The bark was truly more ferocious than any encounter, and I rarely had the occasion to have to run.

Here's the point: when you are pursuing more intimacy with Jesus Christ (and not for His material blessings only), the big dog behind the fence or chained to the pole, Satan, will make a lot of noise like he is coming after you. You should flee his presence to fight through temptation, but you do not have to fear his power!

When God declares that He has plans for you, plans for well-being, to give you a future and hope, you can run to God through your relationship with Jesus Christ. The threats and the anxieties of life may be real, and the big dog may bark, but if God has already declared a thing, it will come to pass!

Two of my favorite passages come up in my spirit:

> Isaiah 54:17 (NASB) says, "No weapon that is formed against you will prosper; And every tongue that accuses you in judgment you will condemn. This is the heritage of the servants of the Lord, And their vindication is from Me, declares the Lord."

> Romans: 8:31 (NASB) says, "What then shall we say to these things? If God is for us, who is against us?"

DISASTER VS. DESTINY

This part of verse 11 is very clear. God says, "plans for your well-being, not for disaster, to give you a future and a hope." Jeremiah 29:11b. This is great news! It reminds me of when we were children.

Our parents always made sure that we had a great Christmas when they could. The anticipation of what we would get had us going to bed at 8 PM and waking up Christmas day at 6 AM!

We never knew what they had planned for us, but it was always good!

I remember vividly one Christmas after my dad retired. That entire year was one big adjustment because of the reduction in finances. My younger brother, Patrick, was still of age to expect gifts on Christmas Day. I remember hearing my mom and dad talking about how this year would be mostly without gifts. Thinking about Patrick, I used money I had made from a part-time job to help buy him a 10-speed bicycle. He was a very happy boy!

While my parents were disappointed about not being able to continue their gift tradition, the gifts that they continually gave us were the gifts of love and care—that made all the difference in the difficult years.

As I think about this, I am reminded of God's love and care. No matter the difficulty or challenge we face in the various seasons of life, we can always count on the love and care of God the Father, Jesus our Savior, and the Holy Spirit, our comforter and teacher.

When I think about the children of Israel's seventy-year exile and why it was that they were in exile, my initial thoughts go to *disaster*, not *destiny!* Think about it—you are relegated to being under the control of your adversary for seventy years because of your disobedience to God, and the One who sent you there is the sovereign God of the Universe.

Sounds like a disaster to me!

But God specifically says, "plans for your well-being, not for disaster, to give you a future and a hope." In other words, God's plans are tied to their destiny and not a disaster!

What does that destiny include?

- Ꮼ Plans for our well-being.
- Ꮼ A future and a hope.

Wow! This is the declaration of God over His children. This is the promise of God that we should remember. I must, however, reiterate once again: *preparing practically* (Jeremiah 29:5-9) to receive and walk in God's plans is a prerequisite.

Just like the children of Israel, we can still recognize that *God's promises are true*!

THE PAIN OF A PROMISE BROKEN AND THE POWER OF A PROMISE KEPT

If you surveyed young, middle-aged, or older adults and asked, "As a child, did you experience one or both of your parents breaking a promise to you?" you would notice an almost immediate change in the person you are speaking to.

If the answer is yes, you will see a change in their facial expression and likely their body language, and they may not want to talk about it. It could be something that happened five, ten, or twenty or more years ago, but the detrimental impact of a broken promise can be felt and transferred for generations upon generations.

Conversely, if you surveyed another group of adults of various ages and asked, "As a child, did you experience one or both of your parents keeping a promise to you?" and they said, "Yes," you would see a big smile show up on their faces, and they would be able to vividly recount the details. On the surface, it may seem like a trivial thing to you, but the power of a promise kept by a parent to a child promotes complete and full trust in that parent.

A PROMISED PLAN KEPT BY OUR HEAVENLY FATHER

As I noted earlier in the book, Jeremiah 29:11 in one of the most researched and quoted verse from the Bible. It is understandably encouraging and inspiring, but left outside of its context, the powerful reassurance found in verses 29:5-14 is easily overlooked. Let's take a moment to dissect and analyze Jeremiah 29:11 within the context we have studied so far:

> "For I know the plans I have for you"—this is the Lord's declaration—"plans for your well-being, not for disaster, to give you a future and a hope."

Please remember that this verse and promise is made specifically to the Children of Israel who are in exile under the Babylonian Empire. As we move forward in the verse. I want to emphasize that my focus will be on the theological truths and how these apply to your life.

God's Love

Although God had exiled them to the control of the Babylonians, His love for them had not changed. This is shown throughout Jeremiah 29 in the directions God had given them. You see, God's love is intrinsic to His nature as found in 1 John 4:7-8 (CSB):

> Dear friends, let us love one another, because love is from God, and everyone who loves has been born of God. The one who does not love does not know God, because God is love.

Because of this, we can be assured of God's love—even when it feels like we have been exiled or placed on permanent punishment. During these times, we can have joy and peace because of the love God has for us. And this love also means that God's specific plans for us will still be revealed in His time.

God's Sovereignty

This simply means that God is in control. He is in control when we are waiting. He is in control when things do not go well. He is in control when we get a bad report. He is in control when things are going great.

God's sovereignty does not mean that adversity, pain, and suffering will not occur in the life of the believer. His sovereignty means that things have to pass through Him before they get to you. And, because He is sovereign, the plans God has for you will come through.

God's Providence

This means God's caring provision for His people as He guides them in their journey of faith through life to accomplish His purpose in them. God's providence would be realized through their obedience to follow the instructions He gave them in Jeremiah 29:5-9. Even in the midst of tests, trials, and triumphs, God's providential hand moves on our behalf. So no matter what comes, stay connected to God because He wants to reveal His plans to you.

Another great example of God's providence is found in Romans 8:28 (CSB):

> We know that all things work together for the good of those who love God, who are called according to His purpose.

Every time I read Romans 8:28, I am reminded of what it takes to bake a cake. The ingredients include sugar, butter, extra large eggs, vanilla extract, all-purpose flour, baking powder, salt, ground nutmeg, and milk.

While some of the ingredients are okay on their own, they make a delicious batter when *all things are worked together.* Conversely, we do not know how what God allows will work out for the good, but because He is the Baker, we know that they will!

I remember hanging around my mom and dad when they would be making a cake so that I could taste that delicious batter. But the cake batter was nothing compared to the actual cake that would be produced after it was placed in the oven for a period of time!

Well, God uses life's oven similarly to providentially work out all the things He allows to work together for the good.

SIGN ME UP FOR GOD'S PLANS!

I hope that this chapter has you excited about the plans God has for you. Please remember that *Some Assembly is Required!* Don't get me wrong—we are not in control, and we should not try to discover those plans on our own. We have to be engaged and actively walking by faith alongside the Holy Spirit for God's plans to be revealed.

We have to be engaged and actively walking by faith alongside the Holy Spirit for God's plans to be revealed.

BUILDING ON YOUR FAITH

The promises and plans of God are true, but we must position ourselves to receive and walk in these promises.

Based on what you read in this chapter, what do you need to do, reflecting back on Jeremiah 29:5-9 and reading through Jeremiah 29:10-11 again, to be better positioned to receive God's promised plans?

Based on what is shared in this chapter, do you now feel better prepared to recognize that God's promises are true?

Always remember that delays do not necessarily mean denial. God's plans for you will come to pass! How will you remind yourself of this when things get challenging?

Go listen to the song *"Watch God Work It Out"* by Candy West—it will truly inspire you.

PRAYER

Heavenly Father, thank You for being a keeper of Your Promises! Thank You that Your love, sovereignty, and providence are there to help us realize Your plans for us. Encourage us to regularly prepare practically so that we are positioned to pursue persistently to receive from You. Help us stay mindful that we are to walk by faith as we pursue persistently. Thank You that You have a destiny for Your children and not a disaster.

In Jesus' Name,
AMEN!!!

CHAPTER 7

REACH OUT TO GOD

*"You will call to Me and come and pray
to Me, and I will listen to you."*

JEREMIAH 29:12 (CSB)

As I begin this chapter, I am reminded of a very painful period in my life. Everything that you'll hear from me I experienced believing no one could understand where I was or the hurt and pain I was going through. Worse yet, I got to the place where I could not even pray.

Yes, you read that right. *I could not even pray.*

Here I am, a licensed and ordained minister of the Gospel since 1994. I had preached to and taught thousands of people. I accepted Jesus as my Savior and Lord in May of 1988. God had blessed me with many leadership gifts to work efficiently and effectively in the corporate world and in His church, but...I could not utter a prayer.

However, I knew that I needed a breakthrough from God, so I was determined to revive the relationally-driven aspect of my relationship with Jesus Christ. Although I could not seem to pray verbally, I took a blank journal, and I began to write out my prayers. I was desperate to talk to and hear from God, and I refused to let anything stand in my way!

The prayers started as one page, and before I knew it, I was writing prayers that were two to four journal pages in length! What a breakthrough! In fact, this mode of *reaching out to God* reminded me of my status before God in 2 Corinthians 4:7-10 (NASB):

> But we have this treasure in earthen containers, so that the extraordinary greatness of the power will be of God and not from ourselves; we are afflicted in every way, but not crushed; perplexed, but not despairing; persecuted, but not abandoned; struck down, but not destroyed; always carrying around in the body the dying of Jesus, so that the life of Jesus may also be revealed in our body.

So, even when it feels like the weight of the world is crushing us and we are unable to pray, we can find a way to keep *reaching out to God* because we are still victorious!

SCOTTY, BEAM ME UP!

Star Trek is a wonderfully done, seemingly timeless series that also gave birth to several movies. One of my favorite parts of the series was when Captain Kirk and Spock would go explore the planet they had landed on. They would go to the transporter room and be kinetically transitioned to the place they wanted to be on the planet.

When it was time for them to go back, Captain Kirk would speak into the communication device and say, "Scotty, beam me up!" Sometimes it would be calm because it was just time to go back. Other times, it was urgent because they were under attack, and they were desperate to make it back.

The fact is, if we stick with the *event-driven* prayer approach of calling out to God, it is almost like we are asking to be immediately "beamed out" of a challenging situation. But if we pursue the *relationally-driven* prayer approach, we can calmly or urgently reach God because we are in regular communication with Him through the power of Jesus Christ's name.

GOD, CAN YOU HEAR ME NOW?

In 2002, Verizon launched a very relatable and trendy ad campaign called "Test Man," starring Paul Marcarelli. You may remember him as the "Can You Hear Me Now?" guy.

Verizon's business grew by over fifteen percent, so it was a very effective campaign. The tagline ended up in late-night show monologues and in our dealings corporately and personally.

Chapter 5 taught us to remember that God cares. Chapter 6 reminds us that God's promises are true. And now Chapter 7 tells us to reach out to God. When was the last time that God heard from you? Was it a two-way conversation, or was it more a one-way, 9-1-1 conversation that frantically asked for help?

Let's take an honest assessment of our pursuit of God through prayer:

Is your prayer life *event-driven*?

Do you only come to God when:

- ✑ Adversity strikes?
- ✑ You get a challenging health report?
- ✑ You're having relational issues?
- ✑ You have a wayward child?
- ✑ You're experiencing financial issues?
- ✑ You're unemployed?

Believe it or not, the truth is that we have all likely fallen into an event-driven prayer life at one time or another.

Is your prayer life *relationally-driven?*

- ✑ Do you have a regular conversation based on your growing relationship and intimacy with God through your relationship with Jesus Christ?
- ✑ An example of what this looks like is found in the Gospel of John, chapter 15, the Parable of the Vineyard. In verses 1-11, Jesus uses the phrase, "Remain in Me" or "Abide in Me" and "I in you" multiple times, which speaks to a growing relationship with Him.

This perpetual engagement with Jesus keeps us from drifting into the *event-driven* prayer life.

HOW AM I SUPPOSED TO PRAY?

Prayer is simply communicating with God. It is important to understand that this communication includes:

- Talking to God
- Hearing from God through His Word
- Sitting quietly before God
- Trusting Him, and
- Walking away in faith knowing that His will is best for us.

I recently wrapped up an eight-week Bible Study that I called "Powerful Prayers." It was an incredible journey with the class as we explored the prayers in multiple circumstances. (It might become my next book!) We started the course with the passage in Matthew 6:9-14, what we traditionally call the *Lord's Prayer.*

When the disciples saw the power that came from Jesus' prayer life with God the Father, they said, "Teach us to pray" Jesus then teaches them what is more correctly called "The Model Prayer." As we walk through this prayer, I want to use some great points that I heard from my Senior Pastor, Lee Allen Jenkins of Eagles Nest Church. Let's look at Matthew 6:9-13:

"Pray, then, in this way:

(Praise)	'Our Father, who is in heaven,
	Hallowed be Your name.
	Your kingdom come.
	Your will be done,
(Priorities)	On earth as it is in heaven.
(Provision)	Give us this day our daily bread.
(Forgiveness)	And forgive us our debts, as we also
	have forgiven our debtors.
(Protection)	And do not lead us into temptation,
	but deliver us from evil.'

Following this pattern will help you develop a consistent way to reach out to God. More importantly, it will help you start and grow a *relationally-driven* prayer life rather than an *event-driven* prayer life.

REACHING OUT TO GOD

In verse 12, God gives us three things that will help us position ourselves to discover His plan for us:

Call out to God.

Have you ever been in a place where you did not know what to do, but you instinctively called out to God? Have you ever cried out and said, "God, where are You?!" Other times, it could be that you are about to make an important decision and you cry out to God saying, "Father, I don't know what to do or where to go; guide me by Your Spirit."

There is a great Scripture in Proverbs 3:5-6 (CSB) that speaks to calling out to God through our obedience to Him: "Trust in the Lord with all your heart, and do not rely on your own understanding; in all your ways know Him, and He will make your paths straight."

Come and pray to God.

Many times, we isolate ourselves from God when things are difficult. We drift away from loved ones and eventually stop serving, stop coming to church, and drop out of our small group. In fact, we have the mindset that no one could possibly understand where we are or understand what we are feeling. But Psalm 139:1-6 (CSB) reassures us that God is omniscient (all-knowing), and He does indeed know what we are thinking:

> Lord, You have searched me and known me. You know when I sit down and when I stand up, You understand my thoughts from far away. You observe my travels and my rest; You are aware of all my ways. Before a word is on my tongue, You know all about it, Lord. You have encircled me; You have placed Your hand on me. This wondrous knowledge is beyond me. It is lofty; I am unable to reach it.

In that same Psalm, King David states that God is also *wherever* (omnipresent) we find ourselves. In vs.7-12:

> Where can I go to escape Your Spirit? Where can I flee from Your presence? If I go up to the heavens, You are there. If I make my bed in Sheol, You are there. If

I live at the eastern horizon or settle at the western limits, even there Your hand will lead me; Your right hand will hold on to me. If I say, "Surely the darkness will hide me, and the light around me will be night"— even the darkness is not dark to You. The night shines like the day; darkness and light are alike to You.

Take courage in knowing that God knows where You are and what you are wrestling with!

God will listen to us.

In the "c" clause of verse 12, God makes an incredible promise: "and I will listen to you." (Jeremiah 29:12 CSB). This is powerful! Think for a minute about the last time you were pouring your heart out to a close friend, but rather than intently listening, they seemed distracted, or they frequently interrupted you.

Those situations are disheartening and frustrating! But God is not this way! As we discussed earlier, it is critical that we develop the *relationally-driven* approach to God in prayer, study, and worship. When we are relationally driven in our approach to God, we can be assured that

When we are relationally driven in our approach to God, we can be assured that He listens to us and that He hears us.

He listens to us and that He hears us. 1 John 5:14, 15 (CSB) gives us a great picture of this:

> This is the confidence we have before Him: If we ask anything according to His will, He hears us. And if we know that He hears whatever we ask, we know that we have what we have asked of Him.

98

Isn't this *powerful?!*

The God of the Universe will make time to listen to us and hear us, and He will reveal His plan to us! So, if we are to discover God's plan for us, we must reach out to God. Don't be discouraged by delays, denials, or disruptions. Instead, continually reach out to God through Jesus Christ.

BUILDING ON YOUR FAITH

All too often, followers of Jesus Christ shrink back from people in their circle and even from God during uncertain times. But in verse 12 of Jeremiah 29, God invites us to do the exact opposite and to reach out to Him.

Based on what you read in this chapter, what do you need to do to break the cycle of shrinking back or isolating yourself and start being relationally driven in your approach to God?

Based on what is shared in this chapter, do you now feel better prepared to reach out to God relationally? If you still need a reminder that God wants you to reach out to Him, check out Hebrews 4:14-16 (CSB). Meditate on His word. How does this encourage you?

> Therefore, since we have a great high priest, who has passed through the heavens—Jesus the Son of God—let us hold fast to our confession. For we do not have a high priest who is unable to sympathize with our weaknesses, but one who has been tempted in every way as we are, yet without sin. Therefore, let us approach the throne of grace with boldness, so that we may receive mercy and find grace to help us in time of need.

PRAYER

Heavenly Father, thank You for inviting us to boldly reach out to You! Help us break the social, emotional, and spiritual cycles of withdrawal and isolation when we are in uncertain times. You have invited us to approach Your throne boldly. Thank You for allowing Jesus Christ to be our relatable High Priest whose sacrifice once and for all defeated death, Hell, and the grave. I pray, God, that everyone reading this book will decide to walk with You and be relationally driven rather than event-driven in their pursuit of You.

In Jesus' Name,
AMEN!!!

CHAPTER 8

REALIZE THAT GOD EXPECTS A WHOLEHEARTED PURSUIT

"You will seek Me and find Me when you search for Me with all your heart."

JEREMIAH 29:13 (CSB)

As shared earlier, I have been very blessed to operate as a Senior Leader in the corporate world for a few companies across multiple industries. I have coached and developed people from entry-level leadership roles who now operate as Vice President and higher roles today.

Each of them was eager to learn, and they showed up as a student every day. I challenged them, gave them stretch assignments, held them accountable, trusted them, coached them, and rewarded them. I also assessed if they were doing the same for their teams. These leaders all had one more thing in common: they approached their roles with wholehearted excellence.

Another way of saying this is they were willing to give 100% or more, consistently.

A WHOLEHEARTED ATHLETIC PURSUIT

After Christmas Break of his freshman year in high school, Myles told me that he wanted to attend the winter workouts for the football team. His high school was at the 7A level. To this point, he had played basketball, baseball, and soccer before playing flag football in the 7th grade, and then tackle football in the 8th grade. The great news is that he made it and played football in the 10th-12th grades. There was something about the required training, preparation, and actual planning that ignited him as a young man.

Myles was incredibly excited about his senior year. He was fully committed to the spring and summer conditioning, and before you knew it, the fall season was kicking off. About three weeks into the season, Myles was hurt. It was first misdiagnosed as an MCL sprain, but after another opinion, it was determined to be an ACL tear.

He was devastated. This was his year—all of the hard work was going to pay off with more playing time and great film to get him a potential opportunity to play at the next level. Myles tried to play and practice on it, but he soon realized that he needed to have surgery in October of 2019.

His recovery process lasted almost a year, but Myles wholeheartedly invested in, and worked through, his physical therapy until it was time to start training again. I can honestly say that I have never seen anyone more dedicated and determined. Not only was his physical and mental preparation impressive, but Myles also began to wholeheartedly pray and pursue God.

Fast forward to today, Myles is juggling his college coursework, staying fit athletically, has helped coach middle and high school 7-on-7 football teams for spring and summer in 2023 and 2024, and is working part-time. It has been a blessing to witness his transformation physically, mentally, spiritually, and academically. Once he graduates, Myles plans to coach and train middle and high school football players. No matter the path he chooses, we love him dearly and are so very proud of the young man he has become.

DANGERS OF PURSUING THE PLAN WITHOUT THE PERSON

I want to pause a moment to reiterate something. Be careful not to pursue the plan as the priority—we must first pursue the God of the plan. Prior to their captivity under the Babylonians, the children of Israel pursued what felt right to them and God became secondary.

There is another passage in the small but powerful book of Haggai. These same people who had been held captive were released to go back to Jerusalem, and one of their main assignments was to rebuild the Temple of God, but they got severely distracted.

Have you ever said, "God, if You get me out of this, I will…" Well, that is kind of what they had expressed. Let's take a look at the dangers of pursuing personal plans while making God's plans secondary:

> The word of the Lord came through the prophet Haggai. "Is it time for you yourselves to live in your paneled houses, while this house [the Temple] lies in ruins? Now the Lord of Armies says this, "Think carefully about your ways: You have planted much but harvest little. You eat but never have enough to be satisfied. You drink but never have enough to be happy. You put on clothes but never have enough to get warm. The wage earner puts his wages into a bag with a hole in it." The Lord of Armies says this: "Think carefully about your ways."
>
> Haggai 1:3-7 (CSB)

God has plans for us, but we must understand that we have to pursue Him persistently to experience the realization of those plans.

As you can see, God did not take kindly to being relegated to second place, especially when He had revealed His plans for them. Verse 13 of Jeremiah 29 shows us that God expects a wholehearted pursuit:

> "You will seek Me and find Me when you search for Me with all your heart."

God has plans for us, but we must understand that we have to pursue Him persistently to experience the realization of those plans. Think about it: if your employer lays out the career progression path that allows you to get promoted over time, and you choose not to participate, you will not experience the fullness of what could be.

If you decide to enroll in a post undergraduate degree and its related certifications, you will not maximize the experience or set yourself up to be hired in that specific field if you pursue it halfheartedly.

If you develop a plan to launch your business, but never follow through on the critical tasks and milestones to build and execute that plan, your entrepreneurial efforts will fail.

ANOTHER EXAMPLE WHERE GOD DEMANDS TO BE FIRST

In the last book of the Old Testament, Malachi, God is challenging His people in chapter 1 to stop giving Him second-hand sacrifices. God also recognized that His people were more attentive to meeting the needs of the government officials and their employers. It was like God was saying, "Hold up. Wait a minute!" Malachi 1:10-11 says:

> "Oh, that one of you would shut the temple doors, so that you would not light useless fires on my altar! I am not pleased with you," says the LORD Almighty, "and I will accept no offering from your hands. ¹¹My name will be great among the nations, from where the sun rises to where it sets. In every place

incense and pure offerings will be brought to Me, because My name will be great among the nations," says the LORD Almighty. (NIV)

Discovering God's plans for us demands that we have a wholehearted pursuit through our relationship with Jesus Christ!

THE BEAUTY OF PURSUING THE AUTHOR OF THE PLANS

Think about it: we can forcibly try to discover God's plans without Him and fail, or we can trust the eternal God of the Universe to reveal Himself and His plans to us when we pursue Him wholeheartedly. After the encouragement to reach out to God in verse 12, now verse 13 tells us:

- ✍ The "What?" We are to seek God.
- ✍ The "How?" We are to seek God wholeheartedly.
- ✍ The "Results?" We will find God when we seek Him wholeheartedly.

This seems simple, right?

Then why is it so hard to pursue God in this manner?

Especially when He has given us the prescribed path?

PUSH PAST THE PREDICAMENTS

Life events happen, and their related pressure can serve as deflators as you try to wholeheartedly pursue God. It is in these situations that we must have a *relationally driven* prayer life with God. It will help us to stand up, dust ourselves off, and keep pursuing God persistently. Listen, disappointments will come, and it is so easy to look at and dwell on the material or moral failures. But we must consistently realize that our wholehearted pursuit of our "El Shaddai" (more than enough God) is worth every encounter with Him.

Be careful! Pursuing something more than you are pursuing Jesus Christ can easily turn that something into an idol. And I am here to tell you from experience, God will not tolerate being second.

Am I telling you not to invest in relationships, your education, starting your business, elevating your career, preparing your children, or strengthening your marriage? No! I am simply telling you that your wholehearted pursuit should be of God—not things, statuses, or people.

I would like to give you some encouragement from God's word as we close this chapter: *don't give up.*

> "So, let's not get tired of doing what is good. At just the right time we will reap a harvest if we don't give up." Galatians 6:9 (NLT)

Aside from accepting Jesus as your Savior and Lord, you will never make a more important decision than to pursue God willfully and wholeheartedly:

- In your personal life.

- In your professional life.

- In your social life.

- In your spiritual life.

Remember, our relationship with Jesus Christ becomes a perpetually growing one. It literally becomes a lifestyle as opposed to a fire drill or an event-driven emotional response.

In Matthew 6:19-34 (NASB), Jesus shows us how to wholeheartedly pursue God first rather than needs or other material things. For our purpose here, I will focus on verses 33-34:

> [33] But seek first His kingdom and His righteousness, and all these things will be provided to you. [34] So do not worry about tomorrow; for tomorrow will worry about itself. Each day has enough trouble of its own.

Jesus gives us the key: *wholeheartedly seek first the King and His Kingdom*. Everything else will be taken care of by God in response. Lastly, and equally important, remember God's promise to us in verse 13 of Jeremiah 29:

> "You will seek Me and find Me when you search for Me with all your heart."

BUILDING ON YOUR FAITH

Wow. God gives us the prescribed path, how we should follow it, and what we can expect when we do. This is a demonstration of the unconditional love and care of God.

Based on what you read in this chapter, how will you begin to apply this truth in your life?

I want to encourage you to take an honest assessment of your life and relationship with God to see what corrections you need to make. Be sure you express a willingness to get back in order. Let your wholehearted pursuit be your priority. God will do the rest and reveal His plans to you.

Based on what is shared in this chapter, do you now feel better prepared to realize that God expects a wholehearted pursuit?

The wholehearted pursuit that God expects can become a lifestyle when we learn to abide by and remain in an intimate and perpetually growing relationship with Jesus Christ as described in John 15:4, 5 (CSB):

> Remain in Me, and I in you. Just as a branch is unable to produce fruit by itself unless it remains in the vine, neither can you unless you remain in Me. I am the vine; you are the branches. The one who remains in Me and I in him produces much fruit, because you can do nothing without Me.

PRAYER

Heavenly Father, thank You for showing us the simplicity of experiencing a growing and transformative relationship with You through our wholehearted pursuit of You. Please allow Your precious Holy Spirit to convict and challenge us when we are tempted to give You less than our best or when we try to relegate you to second place. Remind us that our wholehearted pursuit is not for the plans, but rather, it is the wholehearted pursuit of Your Person. Thank You for Your unconditional love.

In Jesus' Name,
AMEN!!!

CHAPTER 9

REJOICE! GOD WILL REVEAL HIMSELF!

"I will be found by you"—this is the LORD's
declaration—"and I will restore your fortunes
and gather you from all the nations and
places where I banished you"—this is the
LORD'S declaration. "I will restore you
to the place from which I deported you."

JEREMIAH 29:14 (CSB)

In June of 2017, my family and I had weathered some storms, but we were on the other side of them. I had been feeling really sluggish and was unable to work out. At first, I thought it may have been my job (I started a new one in February of 2017), but I was having a great time learning about my new company and industry. One day, I walked in from the parking lot and up two flights of stairs and felt like I wanted to collapse. I went to the onsite clinic, and the physician's assistant gave me a rescue inhaler and encouraged me to go to my primary care physician the next day.

After checking my vitals, they took x-rays, and all the while, I was still struggling with breathing. I was supposed to be in and out and meeting Leslie and Myles while he was trying for his driver's permit. The doctor came in, gave me a copy of the x-ray, and told me to head to the emergency room. My x-ray revealed some type of trauma that frightened them.

The emergency room nurses and doctors tested me for multiple things: Tuberculosis, Legionnaires Disease, Pneumonia, and other potential diseases. The ER doctor told me he did not know what was going on, and I saw Myles tear up. I was stuck in the hospital over the weekend, and I became annoyed with the lack of information. Oh, did I tell you I was in a quarantined room and that everyone coming in and out had to robe and mask up?

I was literally threatening to walk out of the hospital unless someone came to talk to me.

In about two hours, a doctor came to see me—she is still my incredible pulmonologist today—who described what she was thinking. After a bronchoscopy procedure of my lungs, she was able to definitively tell me that it was Sarcoidosis—an incurable autoimmune disease. She told me that the disease could spread to my brain, eyes, more of the lungs (both 33% scarred), and to other organs, and that the only way to treat it was with steroids.

I tried crying out to God, but I could only shed tears. Eventually, I yelled and asked God to heal me despite the report I received. I asked God to reveal Himself and His will to me, but I felt nothing in my spirit.

The next day, I woke up and felt, "My grace is sufficient for you, My power is made perfect in weakness." 2 Corinthians 12:9 (ESV)

Since that day, I have partnered with my pulmonologist, do breathing treatments daily, and work out three to four days per week. I am a leader of a team of fifty people across the country for work. I'm taking care of my family and serving God through our church. Despite what I have to press through, God is still revealing Himself and His plans to and through me, and I praise Him for that daily!

LOST AND FOUND

You wake up a little late. When you are finally dressed, you grab your backpack and head for the door. You suddenly remember that you do not have your keys. Where are they?!

You go back to the place you normally keep them, but they are not there. Frustration kicks in. Where are my keys?! You have a vehicle you really enjoy and care for, but it is just sitting there because you don't have what you need to ignite the power to get to your destination.

Finally, you retrace your steps mentally, going back to when you last had the keys. Then you remember the jacket you wore yesterday and, *voila*, you find your keys. Now you are smiling, and, more importantly, you have the piece of equipment required to ignite the power of your vehicle. This will enable you to get to your destination.

If you go back to Jeremiah 29:1-4, you will find the children of Israel under the captivity of the Babylonian Empire. God had warned them that they would be in exile for seventy years due to their disobedience and refusal to follow His commands and plans.

In other words, they had lost their way. Because they had lost their way, they had also lost the ability to find or hear from God. But now, God deliberately comes to reassure them that He has plans for them. In verses 5-14, God tells them what must be done to realize the plans He has for them:

- *Prepare Practically*
- *Pursue Persistently,*

But now in verse 14, God promises to reveal Himself to those who truly seek Him:

> *"I will be found by you"* – *this is the LORD's declaration...*
> Jeremiah 29:14a

God's promises and our willingness to prepare practically and pursue persistently are the power that will result in God revealing Himself, and they will drive us to discover His plans for us!

HOW DOES GOD REVEAL HIMSELF WHEN I PURSUE HIM?

God promised to reveal Himself when we pursue Him with all of our heart in Jeremiah 29:13. Will we literally see the physical or paranormal manifestation of God? No...

However, when we pursue God with all our heart, we will find Him in many ways. The items below are by no means an all-inclusive list because God has the power to reveal Himself in whatever way He wants to.

So, *rejoice* knowing that God the Father, God the Son, and God the Holy Spirit *will* reveal Himself:

Through Peace
In other words, you will experience a sense of calm right in the midst of chaos.

Anyone need calm in the midst of chaos?

We have *peace with God* because of Jesus's atoning sacrifice, but this passage shows us that we will experience the *peace of God* when we release anxiety.

> Don't worry about anything but in everything, through prayer and petition with thanksgiving, present your requests to God. And the **peace** of God, which surpasses all understanding, will guard your heart and minds in Christ Jesus. Philippians 4:6, 7 (CSB)

Through Joy

Joy is stability on the inside in the midst of instability on the outside. Sometimes we are distracted from what God is doing and revert back to seeking happiness, based on happenings, rather than praising God for the joy that we have through Jesus Christ.

> "I have told you these things so that My joy may be in you and your joy may be full." John 15:11 (CSB)

When we pursue God with all our heart, "the **joy** of the Lord is your strength." Nehemiah 8:10b (CSB)

Through Sufficient Grace

God doesn't always say yes; however, God's sufficient grace is able to help us through all of life's thorns. When we lean into God's sufficient grace, we will experience His presence that will bring us through. Rest in this truth, and God will reveal Himself.

> Concerning this, I pleaded with the Lord three times that it would leave me. But He said to me, "My grace is sufficient for you, for My power is perfected in weakness. Therefore, I will most gladly boast all the more about my weaknesses, so that Christ's power may reside in me. So, I take pleasure in my weaknesses, insults, hardships, persecutions, and in difficulties, for the sake of Christ. For when I am weak, then I am strong." 2 Corinthians 12:7-10 (CSB)

Remember that God's ways and thoughts are different from ours! His all-sufficient grace is available to each of us and the strength of the Lord Jesus is made perfect in our weakness.

Through Provision

When we make Jesus Christ the focus of our search, regardless of what we are looking for, He will remind us that He is THE SOURCE, and that good resources will come as a result of who He is and because of our wholehearted search. God will reveal Himself by giving us provision for our needs and His plans for us.

> "But seek first the kingdom of God and His righteousness, and all these things will be provided for you." Matthew 6:33 (CSB)

Through Effective Prayer

Our prayer life becomes a two-way dialogue when God reveals Himself to us. This level of growing intimacy will also sensitize us to discerning and hearing and receiving the will of God for our lives. Always remember that God's will is *best!*

Always remember that God's will is best!

> "This is the confidence we have before Him: if we ask anything according to His will, He hears us. And if we know that He hears whatever we ask, we know that we have what we have asked of Him." 1 John 5:14, 15 (CSB)

Through Rest

How many of us are waking up mentally, spiritually, and physically exhausted? Even after six to eight hours of sleep. Part of the problem is that we are not resting. As we seek God wholeheartedly, He reveals Himself in a way that provides rest.

> "Come to Me, all of you who are weary and burdened, and I will give you rest. Take up My yoke and learn from Me, because I am lowly and humble in heart, and you will find rest for your souls. For My yoke is easy and My burden is light." Matthew 11:28-30 (CSB)

Through Godly Plans

The truth is that we can sell ourselves on the fact that our plans are properly motivated—*I'm doing it for the Lord*—while in actuality, the motivation for our plans is being driven by the unholy trinity of "me, myself, and I." We can fool others and even ourselves, but we cannot fool God. Thankfully, verse 3 reminds us that God reveals Himself in plans that honor Him.

> The reflections of the heart belong to mankind, but the answer of the tongue is from the Lord. All a person's ways seem right to him, but the Lord weighs the motives. Commit your activities to the Lord, and your plans will be established. Proverbs 16:1-3 (CSB)

Do you want to see God's person and plans revealed to you? Then make Him the primary object of your pursuit—not the plans—and you will experience the power of His plans being revealed and lived through you.

"I will be found by you"—this is the LORD's declaration...Jeremiah 29:14a

BUILDING ON YOUR FAITH

The list of what you will find as a result of God revealing Himself is not intended to be exhaustive. The ways God can reveal Himself to those who wholeheartedly seek Him are infinite!

God wants to do life with us.

Based on what you read in this chapter, how will you begin to apply this truth in your life?

What will you do to ensure you are positioned to experience God revealing His plans and Himself to you?

Based on what is shared in this chapter, what can you do to ensure you are positioned to rejoice and know that God will reveal Himself?

I pray that you will find encouragement through Moses' encounter with God in Exodus 33:16-17 (CSB):

> "How will it be known that I and Your people have found favor with You unless You go with us? I and Your people will be distinguished by this from all the other people on the face of the earth." The Lord answered Moses, "I will do this very thing you have asked, for you have found favor with Me, and I know you by name!"

PRAYER

Heavenly Father, thank You for Your promise to reveal Yourself to us. Help us remember that a persistent, wholehearted pursuit of You will lead to a God encounter, and this encounter will promote a growing intimacy with Jesus Christ. As a result, Your power will flow through us so we can discover and operate in the purposeful plans You have for us. We will REJOICE in this promise and will witness to others about these encounters with You.

In Jesus' Name,
AMEN!!!

PURSUE PERSISTENTLY

Wow! This has been a journey. I want to remind you of what we just covered in Part 2: *Pursue Persistently:*

- ✒ Remember that God cares in verse 10.

- ✒ Recognize that God's promises are true in verse 11.

- ✒ Reach out to God in verse 12.

- ✒ Realize that God expects a wholehearted pursuit in verse 13.

- ✒ Rejoice! God will reveal Himself! in verse 14.

If I had to summarize Part 2 in one sentence, it would be this:

Spend your life pursuing God, and His plans for you will be revealed in His timing.

Take it from me, it is really easy to pursue plans for our lives. The education we achieve, the expertise that we develop, and the success we achieve can all get in the way of us pursuing our God as the priority.

But there is a problem. When we unconsciously pursue the plan rather than the God of the plan, what we achieve will absolutely be temporary, all because we prioritized following the emotions and desires of the *unholy trinity*: me, myself, and I.

TWO OPPOSING PLANS

While this may seem a little random, I want to share one of the most powerful scriptures that speaks to the fact that there are two opposing plans for your life:

> "The thief's [Satan's] purpose is to steal and kill and destroy. My [Jesus] purpose is to give them a rich and satisfying life." John 10:10 (NLT)

It is clear that Jesus Christ came to Earth to be the sacrificial atonement for our sins to restore us in our relationship with God. But His purpose is not limited to eternity.

The statement that Jesus makes in the second part of John 10:10 makes it clear that He has a plan that is in opposition to Satan's plan. The beauty of this is that the plan is to also be experienced in our lives on Earth! We can see proof of this statement by revisiting Matthew 6:9-10 (NLT):

> "Pray like this: Our Father in heaven, may Your name be kept holy. May Your kingdom come soon. May Your will be done of earth, as it is in heaven."

This is why we must always prioritize the pursuit of God over the pursuit of the plan. Our pursuit of God over the human plans without God also means that the Enemy of our soul is not only defeated in eternity but he is also defeated on Earth. Please remember this verse and do not lose sight of what we must do to *pursue persistently*.

Think about this: the eternal Creator of the Universe has specific plans for you!

Aren't you curious? Maybe you are excited. Are you anxious? Are you afraid? There is no need for fear or anxiety. Just rest in the fact that God has specific plans for your life, and He wants you to Prepare Practically and to Pursue Him Persistently. I pray that when you look at Jeremiah 29:11 (NASB) going forward, that you will see it through the eyes of our Savior and Lord, Jesus Christ:

> ¹¹ For I know the plans that I have for you,' declares the LORD, 'plans for prosperity and not for disaster, to give you a future and a hope.'

Whether preparing practically or pursuing persistently goals in your career, your health, your education, your children, your marriage, your family, or your business, it is always best to seek after God first. In Matthew 6:33(NASB), Jesus Christ illustrates this in one powerful verse:

> "But seek first His kingdom and His righteousness, and all these things will be added to you."

You may be reading this and thinking that you see your career, your personal life, your education, and your aspirational goals as separate life compartments and plans. I want to encourage you, however, to understand that having a Christ-centric pursuit as your foundational priority will make seeking God's plans for your life much more satisfying and lasting.

Trust me, I am not writing what I heard someone else say. I am not just repeating information I found in the Bible. I am reaching out to share the benefits of what I have lived out. My story—personal, professional, and spiritual—has turned out in ways I would have never imagined.

Remember, my plans had me owning my own shoe and apparel retail store. God's career plan for me, however, elevated me to the C-Suite even before I went back to college to complete my degree. My spiritual life consisted of going to church occasionally. God's spiritual plan included receiving Jesus Christ as Savior and Lord and becoming a Senior Pastor of a new church for ten years.

I pray that you now have greater insight into *Discovering God's Plans,* and that you have a part in it.

God bless you!

ABOUT THE AUTHOR

A ndré Blythe, the third youngest of eight children, began teaching the Bible in 1992, answered the call to Christian ministry, preached his first sermon, and was ordained in 1994. Over the years, he has served as an Associate Minister, Assistant Pastor, Elder, and Worship Leader in multiple churches, and was the Senior Pastor of a church plant for nearly a decade. André has also enjoyed a thirty-year career as a senior executive leader, leading large multi-site groups in the Financial Technology and HR Technology industries.

As a Senior Pastor, André taught in a multi-week sermon series format. This gave André the writing bug. He frequently refers to Jeremiah 29:11 in his sermons and believes that living the life God has mapped out is more about being faithful to the process than fixating on the end result. His mission is to share that finding God's plan involves both revelation and participation. When not writing or teaching, André enjoys spending time with his wife, Leslie, and their son, Myles, who will graduate from college in the spring of 2025.